Provisional Churches

Provisional Churches

An Essay in Ecumenical Ecclesiology

CHRISTIAN DUQUOC

SCM PRESS LTD

Translated by John Bowden from the French
Des Églises Provisoires. Essai d'ecclésiologie oecuménique,
published 1985 by Les Editions du Cerf, Paris.

© Les Editions du Cerf

Translation © John Bowden 1986

British Library Cataloguing in Publication Data

Duquoc, Christian
    Provisional churches : an essay in
    ecumenical ecclesiology.
    1. Christian union
    I. Title II. Des églises provisoires.
    English
    262'.72   BX8.2

    ISBN 0-334-01338-0

First published in English 1986 by
SCM Press Ltd, 26-30 Tottenham Road, London N1 4BZ

Phototypeset by Input Typesetting Ltd, London SW19 8DR
and printed in Great Britain by
Richard Clay (The Chaucer Press) Ltd
Bungay, Suffolk

Contents

Preface

The churches which only recently were centres of controversy in Europe now evoke no other sentiment than indifference. Every now and then, during the travels of John-Paul II or at a major Protestant church gathering, radio and television are interested in some anecdotal aspects of the existence or folk-lore of the churches. Their message is rarely brought out. Writing about them would seem to be more a matter of naivety or childish optimism. I would not deny this pessimistic view, but my faith is not based on the successes of the churches but rests on the Christ who gave the Spirit. My work as a theologian does not depend on the success of the churches but is buttressed by the reliability of the Word of God. I am well aware of the present difficulties, but I am not resigned to giving in to the Manichaeism which situations of crisis produce, to following the integralists or the fundamentalists in complaining about the disappearance of the certainties and customs of yesteryear, or following the progressives in being irritated at the slowness and ponderousness of the churches in making the changes which are called for by an honest dialogue with the modern world and its ideology. Furthermore, in spite of the present recession in the European churches, I think that a major transformation has taken place over the last decade: the churches have accepted that they are many and varied; they have stopped fighting and tearing one another apart; they have grown used to doing without the conception of unity in terms of a model with an imperialistic centre. This transformation will have considerable effects on relations between the churches and their relationship to the world. I also see this transformation as the source of a new vitality. So, far from despairing of the capacity of the churches to turn the present recession to their advantage, I feel that the changes in their mutual relationships herald another period of expansion.

This observation and this hope have led me to formulate a hypothesis: far from needing to be marginalized as an unfortunate accident of our history, on the contrary the fact that there are many churches forms the starting point for theological and ecclesiological thought. If we forget this empirical multiplicity we tend towards an idealistic way of thinking: and in that case the church that is spoken of is no longer our historical church, as we find it, but its ideal. And it is not far from thinking in ideal terms to imposing norms on concrete reality, or from the imposition of norms to repressive measures. If the ideal church is one and holy, and if this perfection is projected on to an empirical church, the result can only be to excommunicate those churches which have no right to this privileged relationship with the ideal. Our history has illustrated the practical and violent consequences of this way of thinking. So I consider that it is necessary to abandon the classical approach of ecclesiology: it has had perverse effects simply as a result of the fascination exercised by the ideal. I shall not be talking here of the 'church' in itself or the ideal 'church'; I shall be talking about empirical churches. I am a Roman Catholic and I am primarily concerned with the church of Rome, but I can never forget that it is one of the many historic churches, and it is not 'the church' in an absolute sense.

This choice involves not omitting something that is very often passed over in silence, the historical character of the churches and consequently their provisional form. The movement of thought here will not be from the ideal to tangible and concrete facts, but from empirical findings to that to which they bear witness. If one begins from empirical observations, it is impossible to miss out the fact that there are many churches. In an approach 'from above', from the ideal church towards a specific church, multiplicity tends to be thought of as deterioration, the effect of sin. But here I shall not be talking of sin in connection with any empirical church: sin does not relate to a break between the empirical and the ideal but to a break between two empirical presentations. The question of the true church does not arise in connection with the ideal church, which some say is invisible, but in connection with the historic churches. To begin from the ideal is to condemn or to absolutize one's church or to judge all churches sinful. And it fails to take account of the positive value of their multiplicity.

The hypothesis which includes the plurality of churches as a positive value expresses what seems to me to be the orientation of ecumenism. This does not just represent an armistice between the churches, an armistice brought about by their social and political failure since the eighteenth century. In that case, ecumenism would amount to realistic behaviour or a state of emergency: it is useless to tear one another apart since the gravest threats come from elsewhere. In that case the resurgence of the churches in society and politics would be the signal for a resumption of hostilities. I think that the social and political weakening of the churches was a necessary condition for ecumenical developments to go beyond the charismatic inspiration of some believers. But though this condition may have made such a development possible, it does not define it. Ecumenism represents a return of ecclesiological thought and practice to the adoption of a starting point actually at the phenomenon of plurality. Without doubt this plurality is felt as a flaw in the light of the demands of the gospel, but it is felt as a flaw in a specific framework, that of an aggressive or polemical multiplicity. The aim of unity does not call for the abolition of multiplicity: in that case it would be necessary to judge multiplicity bad or perverse; this aim denotes another form of relationship, a form which ecumenical dialogue seeks to define and practise.

Ecumenism has lost its glory. The slowness of the apparatus has disappointed believers impatient for tangible results, who have called it bureaucratic. Those who fought enthusiastically and courageously at the grass roots for dialogue between the churches to get beyond the stage of courtesy feel robbed of the expected fruits of their action.

I can understand this irritation, but I do not share it, even if the bureaucratic apparatus and its calculated caution often get on my nerves. This slowness does not destroy what is at stake. Ecumenism has in fact created an irreversible current; it is a form of theological thought which from now on cannot stop at the boundaries of a single confession or a single historical church. This form of thought, which has emerged from a practice which often precedes the goodwill of the apparatus of the church, undermines the unitary ideology which is closely linked with violence and which has produced so many misdeeds and crimes in the history of Christianity. In doing this it opens the way to another idea of unity, which rules out the use of violence as a means to a visible anticipation of the kingdom in a church. That is the way which I shall try to explore in this book.

Introduction

The retreat of historical Christianity is an event affecting the churches: it is verifiable, since the churches can be empirically observed. By contrast, indifference to the faith cannot be seen in itself, since the term denotes a personal relationship with God: we can only judge its effects, and they are ambiguous. Our methods of investigation are not adapted to grasping truth or personal authenticity. So we are obliged to turn to the churches: they represent the public, historical form of Christianity.

Two objections can be made to this choice. The first, more classical one, has been made particularly by the churches of the Reformation. It recalls that the church is a spiritual reality of which only dogmatics can speak on the basis of scripture; the second, which is more recent, argues that as the apparatus of the church becomes blurred, Christianity must become a social and earthly reality. The theory of secularization represents reflection on the intuition that Christianity is itself as soon as it is no longer separate from the everyday world or social life.

Here, in a more precise form, is the argument used in these two objections.

The first objection is based on a refusal to see the observable history of the church as the specific form of Christianity. It rejects the claim that an ecclesiological theology can be developed from the history of the movement which goes back to Jesus. The church is essentially invisible.

One can appreciate the adoption of this position to the degree that it is directed against the identification of the church with the apparatus of the hierarchy, worship, or the sacraments. It was in fact a tendency of the Roman church, after the break in Christendom, to define the church as a legal institution insulated from the chances of history because it was distinct from the people, but visibly represented by immovable structures by reason of the decision of

1

its founder. Thus the Roman church defines itself by a doctrinal, sacramental and authoritarian structure which cannot be affected by any event or historical transformation.

The rejection of this legalistic picture is not focussed on a rehabilitation of the community, but is organized around a priority given to the grace of God. The church has an invisible essence, and the history in which it has its visible form does not need to be taken into account by theological reflection.

This option does not seem to me to be satisfactory. Certainly I accept that without the gift of the Spirit there would have been no gathering of believers and therefore no church. But I refuse to accept that the historical appropriation by believers of the word of the gospel has no significance whatsoever. Whatever else it is, the church is this deposit of the 'irrational' invitation and the collective response to it. The invitation and the response have a historical effect on the church. This reciprocal influence, for better and for worse, makes the church a living witness and not a structure or a writing. By living witness I mean a witness who reacts. In this sense the church is a historical reality, and because it is the place where scripture is read and interpreted, it is the only place where Christianity takes on a tangible dimension. The elaboration of ecclesiology does not consist in deducing a doctrine from the relevant parts of scripture, but in giving reflective expression to the practices of believers. In short, in interpreting the history of communities which go back to Christ through the mediation of scripture and the recognition of the gift of the Spirit.

The second objection is more subtle: it exalts Christianity at the very point at which it is abolishing the churches.

This objection seems to me to have arisen on the basis of a twofold development: on the one hand, Christianity only achieves its aim when it is not an entity separated from society; on the other hand, the churches are no longer dominant when what they preach as ethical demands have become universally accepted at the level of law. The recession of the churches is the fruit of their cultural success.

The first option presupposes that Christianity is not a religion. It fades away to the degree that people take their destiny into their own hands. Since he is also the creator God, the Christian God calls for independence or responsibility. So Christianity realizes its essence where it inspires civil and political society in an ethical way. Its success ensures its disappearance as a tangible historical form. Thus human rights in the United Nations Charter are inspired by the Bible, in the sense that historically the Bible was the instigating force behind a transformation of social relationships. But once these rights become a common possession of humanity, the adjective 'biblical' is no longer legitimate. The substance is all that counts. Secularization represents a process of appropriation for which the substance of the action matters more than its origin. This option represents an interpretation of the historical stakes of Christianity. It also contains a theological judgment on the role of the churches. That is the second option.

This role is not to assume the direction of society. It was the mistake of mediaeval Christianity to prefer the adjective to the substance, the declaration to reality. The role of the churches is to act as if they no longer needed a separate existence since their ethical and *ipso facto* transcendent aim had been accomplished. Evidently the process of secularization to which the recession corresponds is an unfinished dynamic. A society in which every role of the churches had disappeared as a consequence of an interiorization of their ethical aim would be utopian. The fact nevertheless remains that here utopia regulates the interpretation of the historical role of the churches. In accord with the grace of God these become invisible, since their substance is simply that of a civil society living out ethical imperatives in an almost spontaneous way.

The objection raised by the secular theologies is seductive, but it is too ideological, that is to say it is insufficiently historical to carry conviction. Its main failing seems to me to be the preponderance of the ethical and political aim over the mystical aim. Let me explain.

The theory of secularization which makes the recession of the social power of the churches the condition, if not the cause, of the effective Christianization of the world seems to me to be a fascinating speculation, but one without historical foundation.

First of all it is a fascinating speculation: it represents a metaphorical transposition of the paschal pattern to the historical future of the churches. The death of Jesus was the condition for the gift of the Spirit to all people. By his absence Jesus in effect realizes the universality of his message. By the abolition of his historical particularity he makes himself all things to all people. The metaphor consists in transposing the career of Jesus to the historical churches. With this difference: Jesus chooses the way of 'kenosis' (humiliation); the churches are opposed to it or resigned to it. Events which arise out of the way in which social relationships become steeped in the message that they proclaim compel them to undergo 'kenosis' when instinctively, like any society, they would choose domination or survival. The disciple is not above his master. The death of the churches is the life of real Christianity – that is to say a Christianity which is not the property of particular groups engendering exclusion. So Christianity can only be universal by effacing itself in the form of specific churches: that is the condition of the gift of the Spirit.

Secondly, it has no historical foundation: there is nothing to demonstrate beyond question that the disappearance of the churches from the surface of society helps the birth of Christianity. The phenomenon of the recession of the churches is too complex to be reduced to a single law of intelligibility. It is undeniable that the message of the churches has favoured their retreat. But that this retreat denotes the Christianization of social life is more wishful thinking than a verified observation. There are many factors involved in secularization: they relate to the order of truth, of political and moral practice, of the influence of science and technology. For Christianity and its witnesses, the churches, these have not all had the same effect. In my view two factors dominate this process: on the one hand the preponderance of a practical form of reason (called technical and scientific reason), which has taken the place of a more contemplative intelligence; and on the other hand the fascination of freedom: the rejection of collective reason as a norm of behaviour.

The recession of the church does not have the same significance in both cases.

In the former case the churches find themselves dispossessed of their mythical function of explaining the universe and history. What people had attributed to them as a power to inform and what they had cheerfully assumed to have been this power have become an objection against their historical behaviour. Their dogmatic method has been criticized: it has set up as evident and authorized truths what were only prejudices. The recession of the churches in the sphere of information does not lead to their social disappearance but favours their having a specific function: they no longer have control of all the truth in an authoritarian fashion; they assess themselves by scripture, that is to say by a specific writing, and not by reason, the possibilities of which have been previously defined, reason which is nevertheless judged to be universal. However, this recession of the churches becomes evident against the background of a predominance which is also particular, that of technological and scientific reason. This specific form of reason tends to become the sole legitimate exercising of reason; in our culture it produces imbalances of which our contemporaries are aware. This phenomenon shows that there is no such thing as secularization in itself, but that there are historical forms of secularization. That in contemporary Europe does not correspond, in its approach to the truth, to an interiorization and assimilation of the concerns of Christianity but to the seduction of a kind of reason the capacities of which to explain and produce have proved to be exceptionally powerful: it has furthered, perhaps even caused, the Western domination of the world. This form of secularization does not so much raise the problem of the need for the churches to decline as a condition of Christianization as lead us to ask whether they are incapable of abandoning their dogmatic idea of the truth at the very time when an almost unprecedented form of reason is emerging. Secularization introduces a dilemma into the debate: there is a choice between dogmatic explanation and scientific and technological efficiency. Secularization does not offer another form which today seems to be decisive for the health of the spirit: welcoming intelligence, a free form of relationship to the world. The domination of the churches by science and the resultant recession are contingent historical phenomena: they are not the results of a process immanent in the essence of Christianity; in other words, they are not its necessary effect.

The era of the dominance of scientific reason provoked a thirst for freedom: that is the second element in secular domination. The principle of scientific reason is not to accept as true information that is based on just one authority. It is not the status of the witness which counts but the possibility that anyone may follow the course which gives access to the truth. The scientific method opens the way to democracy; it is a condition of freedom, since it does not recognize any authority which can legitimate its role. Thus the social and ethical effect of the domination of scientific reason was the emergence of freedom as the primary form of the right of the individual. The churches could be obstacles to freedom since they were based on the principle of authority.

There have been long discussions about the capacity of the churches to accept sincerely the freedom claimed by modern people. On this point the churches of the Reformation and Catholicism do not share the same attitude. The former put the stress on Christian freedom and are not afraid to join in the game of church democracy; they construct an ethic according to which the emergence of freedom breaks the yoke of the natural law. By contrast the Catholic church, by virtue of its hierarchical structure, mistrusts the social form of freedom, democracy, and its ethical form, the relativization of so-called natural law. It remains attached to the principle of authority or transcendence, which it believes to be the only one to do justice to revelation, that is to say the irruption of the Other, God. Hence secularization, to the degree that it represents a reappropriation of the power of decision by the individual and the people, seems to it to put in question the aim of Christianity and to make an almost sinful claim. Here the retreat of the churches does not signify the real Christianization of society but paganization. This feeling explains the mistrust expressed in official Catholic texts about the modern world, notably over the question of sexuality, which it sees as the symptom of a freedom that does not want to recognize any norm outside its own pleasure. In this case, the least stress on other spheres would be explained by the fact that here the modern claim to freedom comes up against a limit: the vigour of the struggle against social exploitation in political movements is a barrier to any excess of the principle of freedom. Relationship with the other person intervenes here as a norm external to individual freedom. In that case secularization in the socio-political sphere would represent a possible Christianization, and the retreat of the churches an effective condition of it.

The aim of these remarks was to demonstrate how secularization has a variety of meanings; how it has a contingent and therefore historical character. They equally prompt reflection on the historical and therefore contingent character of the churches by analysing their modern recession.

A dogmatic approach to the churches comes to a dead end over their historical future. The dogmatic approach finds in scripture the view that it proposes for the church. Images like 'people of God', 'body of Christ', 'temple of the Spirit', and so on, the parables in the Gospels, the beginnings of structures for the communities in the Epistles provide the material which allows an ecclesiology to develop. But these images, which play the role of normative ideas, are not tested by the historical reality of the churches as they are. It is out of the question for this method to move from the biblical image of the 'people of God' to its theological concept by putting it to the test of history or sociology. So the theological concept is based on the need for a subject who issues a call: God convenes, and those who are convened form his people. The determination is structural, although it cannot be demonstrated, since in the religious sphere every tangible norm tends to become a factor of intolerance. To specify who is convened outside the universality of the calling is to risk 'judaizing'. Thus history is evacuated of meaning at the level of theological reflection so as not to make a visible community significant in such a way that the slogans about salvation which come from scripture become regressive rather than liberating affirmations. We are familiar with the ideological use of the slogan 'No salvation outside the church'. All the effort put into ridding this slogan of its intolerant connotations has consisted in detaching the church from visible realities. In this way it has proved possible to develop the theory of anonymous Christians. I respect the concern which explains these interpretations but I do not accept their effects, the construction of idealist ecclesiologies. By 'idealist' I mean ecclesiologies for which the future of the churches which is empirical, effective, analysable and therefore historical has no theological significance. The custom of attaching the adjective 'invisible' to the noun 'church' encourages timidity: it is an incitement not to be concerned with the reality of Christian history. No one knows what the invisible church is if there are no demands which its utopian character makes on Christian groups. The invisible church is in fact an eschatological concept; it is consequently a critical element in an analysis of the empirical churches which prevents them from being identified with the kingdom of God. What we are to consider theologically is not the invisible church but the changing, conflicting relationship between the empirical (the visible churches) and its critical point, the eschatological concept (the invisible church). To build an ecclesiology just on the concept of the invisible church is

7

to introduce an eternitarian ecclesiology and to leave out the relationship to history which gives our churches a contingent or provisional character.

The churches can in fact be seen as a collective and often conflicting dynamic arising out of the association of men and women around a conviction about a certain Jesus of Nazareth – a conviction which goes with a project about the significance of human existence and which is buoyed up by a hope towards and against everything.

The history of these groups of believers can partly be analysed, since we have documents about them. There is no way in which we can call it ideal: it was marked with distressing conflicts; it was the context of choices both fortunate and unfortunate; it bears witness to serious defects and errors of judgment; and throughout it heroism and honesty can be found as constants. Whatever may have happened, and whatever may still happen, this eventful history still continues to offer hope. The hope is not always unambiguous, since the promise fluctuates between this world and the beyond. The churches often favoured the beyond at the wrong time, seeming not to be interested in our history of violence. At times they have been the scene of such turbulence that they have brought other social relationships into being, thus shifting the promise towards this world. The churches remain faithful to themselves to the degree that they do not reduce to their hesitant dynamic, which is sometimes pedestrian and sometimes enthusiastic, the image which inspires them, the kingdom evoked by the metaphor of the heavenly Jerusalem, the invisible church. Thus Christian groups, witnesses to the faith of Jesus of Nazareth, are marked by the contingency of their history and the provisional character of their situations or their structures. It is this provisional character which lies at the basis of the possibility of an invisible church as a utopian concept. It remains for us to consider the link between the ambitious dynamism of the historical groups which go back to Christ and the emergence of the heavenly Jerusalem. The invisible church ceases to be the ideological justification for a questionable history to the degree to which it takes root in the provisionality and the contingency of the visible churches. Contemporary movements within the churches, often contradictory in their ideals and their practices, confirm this perspective, a perspective which is relative because it is historical, and one that the necessity inherent in theories of secularization tended to conceal.

Introduction

The movement of theology is secondary; it follows the development of experience. The theologies which have produced theories about the recession of the churches have eliminated facts in the contemporary experience of the church. This experience derives from the encounter between the challenge posed by the modern world and a belief that the gospel is relevant to the present day. The fact that over the past twenty years groups have arisen in all the churches which are deeply concerned for the purity of the gospel is not a sign of nostalgia for the past or of an illusion that Christendom can be recreated; rather, it indicates an awareness of urgency. These groups were and are different in the choices they have made: there are anti-establishment basic communities which are more or less politicized; biblical and theological study groups; consciousness-raising groups about the problems of the Third World; groups for liturgical renewal; prayer groups; charismatic groups, and so on. They share a common conviction: the churches cannot be content to be involved in current affairs. The cultural and social setting which ensured the almost natural transmission of the faith is breaking up. Militant Christian parents sadly feel that their convictions are not being handed down. The churches today no longer enjoy the co-operation of family, social and political institutions. Their morality differs from the dominant morality. Their hope would seem far-fetched or mythical. Their faith is thought to be childish or consoling. The recession of tangible faith which all Christians can see around them has finally led many groups to resume contact with the hope and demands of the gospel.

The development of this spontaneous and scattered recourse to the sources of faith crosses that of groups nostalgic for the past, groups described as integralist. The publicity which the mass media has given to some of them in France has increased their numbers. These groups have given the impression of being a major force. In fact they have a negligible recruitment, their audience is limited and their problems are too anachronistic for them to count much in the effective future of the churches. It would, however, be a lack of discernment to overlook the symptom which they represent. Fundamentalists in the Reformation churches and integralists in the Catholic church betray the same obsessive fear: that the faith is no longer presented in a clear social and scriptural framework. The mutations which have developed heighten the sense of insecurity that their attitudes betray. These believers look for unmistakable reference points in social ritual or scriptural evidence: they would not know how to obey God if there were no evidence of his will. The historical variations of scriptural interpretation, changes in the liturgy, the destabilization of ritual, the transformation of hierarchical relationships seem to them to decentralize faith, to fragment it into a thousand contradictory possibilities, and as a result to rob it of all power of persuasion. Thus fundamentalism and integralism are the signs that a society is living dangerously, uncertain of its identity and its own aims.

The public for these groups is minimal, but the malaise that they reveal is very widespread. The regular administration of the churches treats this discontent as 'popular religion'. Christian intellectuals have thought that it is contrary to the gospel; they have also urged the church to accredit faith and to devalue religion. Here the urgency for conversion to the gospel is taken seriously, but in a rigorist framework which eliminates the evangelical turbulence that secretly inspires popular religion. It would have been a shame for the Catholic church not to be interested in places of pilgrimage, attracting great crowds, or to prohibit demonstrations of the faith in South America on the pretext of purity. That would be to be deprived of popular roots and a form of expression suited to a number of believers. A healthy treatment of popular religion will work to detach it from the integralist pathology: a refusal to listen to the request inherent in this form of expression favours anachronistic closedness.

The experience of the church today is made up of this fragmentation among different groups or sensibilities. The boldest of them bear witness to a vitality inspired by the gospel which will not take as its starting point the slow death of the community by dissolution into the surrounding society: they judge that without the ferment of the gospel this society would succumb to demons which are already too active. The more sensitive are perhaps more aware of the deadly peril threatening the churches, but fear prompts responses in them which, stressing the sectarian aspect, would lead believers to external exile, as witnesses to a society in process of disappearing. The great majority hesitate between a boldness which often excites them and a fear which makes them anxious. It is not easy to cope with this hesitation: to make people afraid as a result of too rapid changes runs the risk of increasing the anachronistic tendency; to go forward

10

too slowly and in too measured a way would discourage those who are impatient to see the churches take part in the dynamism of our modern world without being its prisoner.

The Second Vatican Council was the courageous witness to these hesitations. In its time the traditional approach was still favoured by a dominant majority. But already, among the mass of believers, there were indications of a new spirit: it was necessary to take note of the transformation of the world, to break the bonds of doctrine, discipline or morality in which the fear of modernity had imprisoned the Catholic church. Theologians had opened up the way to a reinterpretation of this church; they demonstrated that the rigorously hierarchical and legalistic organization of Catholicism was a recent creation; they had the ear of movements like Catholic Action, born out of the appeal of Popes to the laity. The revolution brought about by Vatican II in doctrinal matters, in relations between churches, in ways of understanding the world, in the break with political conservatism, seemed so considerable that the effect produced was not so much a reform as a destabilization or an explosion.

But explosion is not the acceptance of a recession. The explosion is the social condition for transformation. This is evidenced by efforts to renew Catholicism by recentring it on the original character of the gospel. If there is an explosion, it is because this originality is not handed down in a legalistic text the rules of which need only be applied or transposed. The original character of the gospel lies in a relationship which is ongoing because it is bound up with the life of the society in which it arises. Our society is no longer that of Palestine at the time of Herod or Pilate. The most rigorous investigations of the behaviour of Jesus in this society will never prescribe for us in an unambiguous way what behaviour the gospel requires in the face of the challenges which we face at the end of the twentieth century. Moreover the present explosion is healthier than the monolithic unity which is often desired. The explosion draws attention to two limits: submersion in world society to the point of abolishing all distance from its ideals, forms of behaviour and goals, or separation or exile from it to the point of no longer having anything to do with it under the pretext of purity. The government of the churches no longer seems to me to be possible without taking account of this explosion: it is the sign that the gospel is not without its ties to our world.

Two courses have led us to a new appreciation of the witnesses without which there would be no memory of the gospel. The first leads to an eclipse of the churches: they have to disappear in order to be conformed to their vocation, since their disappearance is the condition of the Christianization of society. This theoretical course is put in question by a second route, that of church practices, diverse and opposed, which are nevertheless all concerned that the churches should not disappear, even if this should require radical reforms. This latter course, which goes against the theological course, has all the more force today as we assess the illusory character of the theory of secularization as latent Christianity. It is because I take the second course that I think it useful to measure its consequences by trying to rethink ecclesiology.

In this book I shall not follow the ways opened up by the theologians who inspired the dogmatic Constitution on the Church, *Lumen Gentium*, which was promulgated at Vatican II. I do not deny that this constitution was a considerable advance on the dominant Catholic ecclesiologies of a legalistic type dating from the first half of the twentieth century. However, I think that its deductive dogmatic character hides the historicity of the church and risks promoting what I have called an idealistic ecclesiology. The plan which I have adopted is more inductive: I shall begin from historical and institutional evidence and then go on to critical or normative images. Thus after a study of the historicity and institutional character of the church I shall show how the qualities which believers confess about it – that it is one, holy, catholic, apostolic – force us to introduce eschatological or utopian concepts without denying the necessary provisionality of the churches as they are. I shall end the book with an attempt at a practical definition of the church from what may be called the 'symbolic' aspect. I hope that the course I have indicated will enable me to bring fully to light the fact that the social witnesses to the gospel are true to their calling only if they accept their provisional character.

I

The Churches and History

For the observer who is not a believer, the churches represent groups of men and women who make public proclamation of their conviction that Jesus of Nazareth – presented by the New Testament as an incomparable prophet – is the Messiah expected by the people of Israel, that after his unjust death he was raised by God and thus established by him as the giver of the Spirit and master of history. This conviction is presented in the cultic, moral and social practices which allow the observer to discover the common features of the attitude of Christians and to distinguish them from the way in which other religious groups believe or live.

What can thus be perceived by the observer who is not a believer is not disputed by the faithful: the churches are an empirical historical entity susceptible of rigorous description and analysis even by those who do not adopt the validity or truth of their message. They are there for all who want to look at them. But the faithful are disturbed about the lack of spiritual depth in the empirical vision. They think that the reality of the churches or their truth is different, that it is invisible. Only the heart can perceive it. The observer who does not make the conviction of faith his or her own, the one familiar with cultic, moral or social practices, the unthinking member of the group into which he or she has been born and educated, who does not enter into the incessant movement of conversion, see only the external apparatus or a social impact of the churches unless they enter into the incessant movement of conversion. And while the faithful who want not only to join in worship and practise morality but to participate in the dynamic of a church may not scorn the empirical, they are anxious to go beyond it to arrive at the invisible, what the New Testament calls the 'kingdom of God'.

The drift towards the invisible, implying the judgment that what is experienced in the churches, their empirical dimension, is not part of their truth, fails to see a structural dimension, their historical character. For the Christian groups have grown out of a break with official Jewish religion; their history and their tradition cannot be confused with Jewish history and tradition but are different. This otherness felt in the empirical entity or historical experience goes back to a tangible separation. To base talk about the church primarily on the invisible reality is to lack a sense of this original break and the other breaks which have come about in history: they too structure the churches. The view of the outside observer is not accidental or made in bad faith: it perceives something essential about the reality of the church. The believer must accept it, not lightly sweep it to one side. This explains why the starting point for my reflection is not the mystery of the 'church', but the empirical or historical character of the churches.

1. The reasons for the choice

Several factors have led me to choose this course: the present crisis, the break-up of unity, the discrepancy between prophetic vision and social practice, theological doubts, 'revivals'. These elements, which I shall outline briefly, will lead me to try to take the historical character of the church or, to put it in a more scholarly way, the historicity of the church, as being fundamental to it.

The present crisis

The first element which leads me to posit historicity as the structure of the churches is the present crisis.

Believers judge that there is a crisis because they can see tangible effects on the stability and vitality of the contemporary churches. Let me list several indications which have been discovered through surveys or quantified by statistics: the decline in baptisms and marriages; the decrease in churchgoing particularly among the young; the flood of resignations from the clergy, the religious orders and the pastorate; the low recruitment for the priestly ministry; dissatisfaction with the formulas of faith and the moral tradition and with the authorities behind them; a lack of cultural vitality in the churches against a background of vigour in contemporary ideas, and so on. These indications betray hesitations in the churches because they reveal creeping doubt about their aims and means. They allow us to understand the indecision of the authorities better. To ignore this situation in working out statements about the church on the grounds that the reality of the church is invisible is to lack the need for discernment, to refuse to take part in the provisional dimensions which determine its audience and its future. To accept this crisis is to try to interpret the churches as they appear, and not as they are dreamed of.

The break-up of unity

To refuse to dream leads us to consider the second element: the break-up in unity. For long centuries the division of the churches was regarded as a sinful effect of the conduct of some of them towards the one true church. For Roman Catholics there was no other church than the Catholic church. Groups which based their authority on the name of 'church' were going beyond their rights: they were wrong in calling themselves defenders of the faith. They had broken up an earlier church unity, but this unity, though damaged, was to be found in the Catholic church by reason of the witness borne faithfully to Jesus Christ by the episcopate in communion with Rome. All those who did not share this conviction were declared heretics or schismatics. The empirical break-up of unity was only one of the many consequences of the sin of believers. So it was to be thought of in the framework fixed by the transcendental scheme of sin and grace; it did not affect the church in its being. Little by little, the practice of ecumenism has blurred the lines of church membership. There has been a transition from war between Christians to negotiation. This change in behaviour represents a shift in judgment: ecumenism is impossible without relativizing one's own point of view. If classical war is postponed negotiation, a war of religion is a total war: the heretic or the schismatic must be converted; there can be no question of compromise. To negotiate is to recognize that the other party has some justification for its position. To negotiate is to join in the game of compromise. One does not negotiate with evil or sin; one destroys it. To negotiate is to recognize the right of the other Christian to confess that the status of his or her church is different. Hence the break-up of unity must be regarded in a less dogmatic way. The churches are separated, they have different experiences, it is now out of the question to suppose that their diversity is simply the result of sin: that is part of their historicity, in other words say a pluralist acculturation of the fact of Christianity.

This pluralistic appropriation of the gospel has to be thought of in terms of a promised unity of which we can now see no more than fragments or anticipatory signs. The aim of the wars of religion was to ensure the promised unity by identifying it with the unity given to an empirical church. Every church orchestrated this claim, each of them feeling impelled to bring the other to its senses. Ecumenism has arisen out of the renunciation of this claim, because in the end it was thought to be against the gospel. But to abandon a transcendent judgment on the separation of the churches leads to a positivistic history or a pragmatic attitude unless another idea of unity goes with the conversion to negotiation. There is a condition for the emergence of this other way of thinking: acceptance of the divisions as facts to be interpreted against the background of the promised unity and a renunciation of any condemnation of them with reference to a unity which has been already perceived empirically. This manner of thinking makes it possible to evaluate the role of the empirical churches, even in their separation, in terms of the construction and expectation of the promised unity. It seems to me impossible to consider the phenomenon of Christianity broken up into multiple churches without taking into account the historical character of the churches.

The discrepancy between prophetic vision and social practice

Christianity broken up into a plurality of churches expresses another form of discrepancy: the difference between prophetic aim and social practice. The phenomenon is too well known for us to need to spend long on it. The Christian churches, heirs to the prophetic tradition, are signs of the promised city. They have this role not by virtue of their invisible character (the term 'signs' is only meaningful in experiential terms) but by their visible witness. Luke describes the first Christian communities as places where relationships were brotherly and just: common sharing of goods has been remembered, and this was certainly voluntary. These idealized descriptions of the primitive church were of interest in showing what Christianity was about: making in the declining world the mark of

16

the 'already there', what could be empirically grasped of the promised kingdom. The visible church is its anticipatory sign.

The truth of such a project rests on the authenticity of the practice that goes with it. Here two elements in putting the vision into practice produce an imbalance: proselytism and idealism. I deliberately leave aside sin: that is invoked in connection with the history of the groups where there is no reasonable explanation.

Proselytism consists in introducing others, whether by persuasion or by constraint, to the group of believers or the community with a view to snatching them out of the perverse world. The prophetic vision, the proclamation of the city of brothers and sisters, is given a different direction since it becomes justification for not respecting others. The intolerance which has reigned in the churches was not primarily the result of a sinful perversity but followed from a zeal for the salvation of others. This zeal was inevitably misdirected once it was buttressed by the city which anticipated the ultimate kingdom. It was impatience for the city of brothers that provoked the madness of persecution or the compulsion of proselytism. The messianic politics of the twentieth century provide us with numerous examples of this perversion of zeal for the welfare of others.

By idealism I understand the conviction that good behaviour or good ideas necessarily have beneficial results. This conviction does not take account of the ambiguous effects of all behaviour and all ideas. Our era, in which people have paid homage to the idol of rational and quantifiable planning, has witnessed numerous bad effects that have been produced by rationally good ideas. What can be verified at the level of social or individual relationships can equally be verified for the empirical churches: the sanctity of the idea or the behaviour does not prevent it from having unfortunate effects. Virtue, or a good idea, is only one element among others in whether a decision, a form of behaviour or a policy proves to be beneficial or otherwise. It is too easy to judge the discrepancy between the prophetic vision and inauthentic practice in terms of sin or immorality. It is neither the sinful excesses of Christians nor the faults of clergy which produce the most problems but the perverse effects of the moral order, or the unforeseen effects of zeal for salvation. The historical character of the churches is seen better in the ambiguity of their anticipation of the kingdom than in the immorality of their initiates. The theologians have spent too much

17

time on the question of evil and have neglected the collective excesses caused by a passion for the Book or impatience for the kingdom. They are nowadays more hesitant about the intelligibilty of the empirical churches.

The hesitations of theologians

After the blossoming of Catholic ecclesiology in the decades before Vatican II, we have seen a theological and ecclesiological void. The theologians from before the Council drew attention to the lack of equilibrium in Catholic theology. Contrary to the intuitions of the theologians of the early and mediaeval church, this was organized around the idea of hierarchy. This stress on the legalistic aspect, circumscribing the church's mediation of the priestly ministry, forgetful of the equality of believers by virtue of their participation in the universal priesthood of Christ through the gift of the Spirit, arose out of struggles against the Protestant Reformation. The Catholics accused those who took this line of having repudiated the institutional form willed by Jesus out of a preference for democracy and egalitarianism. They also concentrated their reflections on this aspect to the point of forgetting the mystical truth of the church. The result was a hypertrophy of the legalistic character of ecclesiology, with a concentration of reflection on those who held power. Moreover apologetics, that is to say the effort made to legitimate the institution of the church in terms of its origin in the gospel, directed its attention to the authenticity of the qualifications of the Catholic church for its authority. In short, theology took the church as its object, it focussed itself on the defence of the authorities and powers of the institution, rejected charismatic dynamics as an exception and accorded believers only the status of obedient subjects. In this theology the church appears more in the image of an army ranged in battle under the banner of the Roman pontiff than as a symbol of the peaceful and open city.

The obsession with legalism, aimed at legitimating authority, lost its fascination once the strategy of the Counter-Reformation proved ineffective in a world that was becoming secularized. No longer was the issue disputes between Christians but the rejection of Christianity or indifference to its sphere. Moreover, the increasing degree of democracy in politics, the desacralization of the authorities and powers, the judgment made on their competence and actions, told against an ecclesiology which was essentially hierarchical. It became increasingly intolerable to think of a disjunction between the dynamics of secular societies and those of the society of the church. The first breach in the hierarchical edifice seems to me to have been opened up by reflection on the laity as an active subject in the church. Theologians[1] recognized that the laity were responsible for church policy in matters of evangelization or witness. This break allowed a shift in ecclesiological reflection: the latter rid itself of the weight of hierarchical authority as a last authority and organized itself around the great biblical images, particularly that of the mystical body. Thus the decades preceding Vatican II witnessed the birth of a minority theology which took account of the tradition of the early church without undermining the predominance of an official theology. Official theology made an effort to recover or render harmless (cf. the encyclical *Mystici Corporis* of Pius XII) the themes developed by this theology which was then in a minority. Vatican II brought about a complete reversal: in principle it adopted the ideals of the minority theology, which thus became official, but it did not open up any space for creation; by contrast – though this is no small achievement – it produced a controversial theology which did not find a place either in the minority theology of the period before the Council, or in the official theology of the period after the Council. The roots of this unsatisfactory position seem to me to lie in the inadequacy of the minority theology of the time – it was inadequate because of its polemical and antagonistic aspects – and in the compromise made at Vatican II.

This inadequacy of what was once a minority theology arises out of its tendency to be reactionary: on the basis of tradition it claims the right of the laity to be responsible agents and legitimates this claim with an appeal to the mystical essence of the church. This argument stops half way: it does not really give the hierarchy a new role in the historical church, so it produces an impasse over the historical and institutional structure of the church. The appeal to the mystical essence does not allow the political problem posed to the Catholic church to be settled. This is so true that the theology of the mandate[2] allows the ancient hierarchology to take in the idea of the 'responsible laity' without changing in the slightest the legalistic structure which gave powers and authorities their legitimation. Because of the numerical lack of clergy, the laity were

19

mandated to play a role which did not devolve to them as of right: it was granted them by delegation. This recovery would not have been possible had the minority theology thought in different terms about the historical and legalistic constitution of the church on which its claim to power and authority was based. The impasse which arose at this point, in reaction to the earlier theology, failed to take into account precisely what should be thought if one wanted the laity to be more than simply 'subject'.

Vatican II did not avoid this difficulty. In the constitution *Lumen Gentium*[3] the reversal brought about in favour of the mystical essence of the church does not go with a convincing effort to articulate the historical and legal aspect. Granted, the hierarchy does not have pride of place in the text, but the restrictions that the facts about the hierarchy impose on the practice of the ministry bear witness to only a superficial change. So it is not surprising that the theologians who support a community ecclesiology and the defenders of a hierarchical ecclesiology find good reasons for their opposite views in the selfsame text of Vatican II. The recent debates on the ministry have illustrated this ambiguity in the constitution *Lumen Gentium*.[4]

This observation is not a criticism of the text. The text was the result of negotiations; it is a compromise. It was fully justified to edit it in this direction, but it is readily understandable that once Vatican II opened up a different situation in the church the compromise text was no longer adequate for considering or interpreting the community movements which have appeared since it was produced: these movements represent a revival in the church. This revival is the last indication I have chosen to show the need to introduce the historical character of the churches into any study of them.

The revivals

The subsequent history of the Catholic church and, specifically, facing up to the problem of the diversity of minist.ies and the articulation of the request by communities for autonomy over against Roman centralism has shown the weakness of the compromise. To think of the Catholic church at a mystical level, to maintain without sufficient articulation at this high profile a hierarchy with discretionary power, to ignore the contingent character of some church decisions in history, to forget the often ambiguous role of

than describe the contingent character of the event.
indicates, rather, that the event has left a trace and
made a mark on a subsequent reality. From this point
very event is historical, since not every event leaves a
a matter of detail.
eft is twofold: the organized or instituted group and

ion of the Christian group from the Jewish movement
became a historical event because this group made its
cultural, social and political environment to such a
ne day it reduced the pagan world to insignificance.
ay be said to be historical by reason of its institutional
ace that can be detected from its ongoing existence.
ure is bound up with the mission that the group
– the handing down of scripture. This makes history:
icular event of Jesus takes on a universal dimension.
the words of Jesus out of everyday conversation and
above local interests. Scripture tends to make Jesus
it defies death.
iderations are justified, then 'historical' denotes the
sed on contingency. The fact 'Jesus' is contingent,
an group which takes its place around scripture in
it on makes it necessary. The actions, conduct and
are no longer anecdotal: they concern every human
come historical by the witness which comes into
w on they are an indisputable trace of the dynamic
he first events. So a historical religion cannot be
an institution, since the latter prevents the contingent
g swallowed up in forgetfulness or death. History
are the essential factors for understanding the
that we call church.
nstitutions are inseparable for a group if it is true
result of efforts undertaken to master contingency.
an accidental quality of the church: it relates to its
rthly church.
misunderstanding, let me make it clear that by
storical character' I mean that such a given reality,
urch, has no essence outside the temporal construc-
s of itself as a result of challenges from within and

the institution, is in the last resort to develop an idea of the church and not to interpret the Catholic church as it exists in history. The ecclesiological void which emerged after Vatican II in fact stems from the fact that the ecclesiologies given official recognition corresponded more to the development of a certain idea of the church than to reflective study of the historical churches with their diversity, their quarrels, their separations, their errors, their contradictions and their revivals. These last represent an alternative movement in the centralized institutional church. Moreover what a number of grass-roots Christians are calling for is not the development of an idea of the church, even if it did come out of the New Testament, but the exegesis or interpretation of what is in fact happening in the churches. As to the hesitation of the theologians or their silence, these are because of the novelty of the direction that thought must take from now on: 'the historicity' of the church in the plurality of the churches. It is no longer primarily a matter of the rights of the laity, the diversity of ministries, the legitimacy of basic communities, of political Christianity, of the invisible and spiritual essence of the church. It is indeed a matter of all that, and much more, but from a dimension which makes it possible to articulate them otherwise, as elements or materials of the church. Neither biblical imagery elevated too hastily to a conceptual level, nor an appeal to the invisible essence of the church, nor the shrivelling up of the institutional structure, allows this articulation: it requires that all the material or the elements should be detached from their historical mode of existence.

2. A reversal of perspective

This orientation is not a return to pre-conciliar theology. Some people may well imagine that not to depart from the mystical reality of the church is necessarily to give either the institution or the hierarchy pride of place, but I want to demonstrate that this is not the case.

Not to start from the mystical reality of the church is to reject the ideal as a rule of interpretation but not to reject it as a critical question. The mystical reality of the churches expresses the aim of which believers must never lose sight, the kingdom. But reflection cannot ignore the difference that there is between this mystical reality and the historical churches. There are two ways of overcoming this distance: identifying every church with the invisible church and not worrying about its visible forms, or ensuring that the institutional and the legalistic elements have such a mediatory value that the structures are the immutable forms of the invisible church which can be seen in our history. So one can talk about the church in a mystical or legalistic way without touching on the question of its mobility; the mobility, that is to say, of its history. For the mystical is not opposed to the legalistic if this latter is understood as a visible reproduction of the eternal will of God. On the contrary, mystical and legal are distinct from historical. That is why not to begin ecclesiology with biblical imagery does not necessarily end up at the pre-conciliar hierarchy of the church. It is not the order that matters here but the function. Now what shifts the movement of reflection is not whether the mystical or the legal is given first or second place in the order of composition; it is whether they are linked by means of a third element: history affecting the church in its totality, that is to say in its pluralistic formulation, since it denotes both the mystical and the legalistic.

The biblical images which suggest the mystical quality of the church are not of immutable essences: they play the role of symbols denoting the reality of the church. They do not suggest that this reality is not empirical, that it is transcendent and in no way affected by the movement of societies; they put a stamp on it which marks it out as not being exhausted in a function or role which can be described. However, this stamp is itself affected by shifts in empirical reality: the function which Paul gives to the image of the mystical body is not exactly that understood by Pius XII. The empirical reality of the church is not identical in each case: the interests are not the same. Nor does the image have the same function. The mistake would be to think that the Bible puts forward a collection of images which have an unchangeable meaning and are applicable in an identical way to every era. They are nothing of the kind: the function of the image alters and transforms the equilibrium of its content by reason of changes in its point of reference, the empirical and plural reality of the church.

This same phenomenon affects legalistic concepts. To consider them immutable would be to mistake their meaning. Thus in its abstract form the prohibition against ordaining women to the

priesthood remains the same; legalistic concept when referr Catholic church. Hence it did has today. The variation in th the concept and the empirical to the point of reversing their the only immovable truth is form, thought of without an mystical evocation or legalist rise to the same error: not to develop the image that is con

If one rejects the mystical of interpretation of the empi to find a context for the thi that the two others had ta historical element affects th it. So we still have to establ original way.

There is one conviction b ianity is a historical religion it goes back to a founder like Islam, has an origin w correct: Christians form recognizable over time th of a certain Jesus whom thought that he was dead

This trivial sense, whi is not primary when one in the complex of proble calling Christianity histo the contingent and parti in fact there is no way o within Christian faith, t Nazarene in the first ce term historical denote event in relation to the of the harmony of faith which is not necessary

can do more
The adjectiv
therefore ha
of view not
trace. So it is
The trace
scripture.
The separa
was a fact: it
mark on the
degree that o
This group m
structure, a tr
This struct
acknowledges
with it the par
Scripture take
raises his actio
contemporary
If these con
necessity imp
but the Christi
order to hand
words of Jesus
being. They b
being; from no
immanent in t
separated from
trace from bei
and institution
empirical realit
History and i
that history is th
Nor is historicit
essence as an ea
To avoid any
'historicity' or 'h
in this case the ch
tion that it make

from outside. So there is no way of getting back to a definition or a pure essence of the church: there are functions and situations which by the interplay of their relationships go to make up the earthly church. The church is not other than that which presents itself here and now, if by 'other' one means an 'ideality' apart from its manifestation. In this sense its institutional aspect, its utopian aim, its mystical vitality, its plural forms belong to the historical character of the church. It is pointless to separate the institutional, divided and variable forms of the church which describe its presence in our world from an essence or pure idea of the church. These brief comments should be enough to establish that I am rejecting an ecclesiology inspired by an alleged original purity and that I am distancing myself from an ecclesiology defined by mystic purity.

Ecclesiology based on the myth of original purity is a weapon for Catholicism: its aim is to criticize the contemporary situation of the church. So it implies that those who hold this theology think that the Catholic church is being unfaithful to the witness of the gospel, and also describe its history in terms of degradation. They issue a call to return to the New Testament sources in order to discover there the model for every church.

The course adopted by H.Küng[5] in developing his ecclesiology is related to this way of thinking. It is certainly a stimulating approach, but it is too timid: it does not come to grips with what must really be taken into account, historical entropy.[6] If the church is originally pure and transparent in essence, time is pernicious for it. By going back in time we rediscover its native vigour. Paradoxically, Küng takes over the process of Platonist remembrance, the negation of history, and the Rousseau-like quest for the original transparency.

In my view this return to origins is illusory: there is no such thing as the essence of the church; there is a church of the New Testament period. The return to origins conceals the unacknowledged quest for a concrete norm or model; it conceals a form of 'positivism'. Therefore any departure from the New Testament would be a matter for condemnation. In fact the New Testament offers several models for churches, as Küng has clearly seen: the witness given to the crucified and risen Christ is incarnated in different forms of community. This originally plural situation shows the historical character of the church and condemns the nostalgia of a return to a so-called primitive purity.

I equally reject an ecclesiology of mystic purity. On this point I part company with the treatise on the church written by Y.Congar.[7] Because of an allergy to forms emerging from the Council of Trent which are predominantly legalistic, Congar builds up his work on the qualities attributed to the church by the creed: unity, holiness, catholicity and apostolicity. These qualities are traditionally called 'marks'. Congar interprets them in a mystical fashion. Certainly he discusses them in a sophisticated way, and the historical knowledge to which his work bears witness preserves him from all excesses. However, the result of his development of this approach proves that if one starts from the 'marks' (some of which relate to the legal structure and others to the mystical utopia) it is difficult to do justice to the society which can be discovered in history and claims to bear witness to the originality of the gospel. The failing of the mystical quest is the same as that of the return to origins: it puts forward an essence of the church which one later sees never to have been achieved.

The fact that I feel that I must dissociate myself from these two theological views must not be seen as a denial of their interest or as indifference towards the New Testament. On the contrary, if one recognizes the full historicity of the church it is possible to attach real importance to the beginning: this approach leaves that beginning its particularity and its precariousness, and it denies its normativeness. Thus it is important to know that originally the church had no female ministers. In a theory based on the assumption that initially the church was pure, this situation will be sacralized and therefore fixed. A historical theory will respect it as an issue without making it normative.[8]

As to the attempt at a mystical interpretation, it rightly stresses the utopian character of the qualities attributed to the church by the profession of the apostolic faith. But it tends to omit the link between the ideal aspect of these qualities and their historical forms. In fact they emerge not in themselves but in the context of their historical contradictions. To forget the discrepancy between the ideal and the concrete form leads to the view that these 'marks' are realized in the Catholic church. In that case the theologian cannot avoid submitting himself to an ideological imperative, that is to say to the actual and supposed interests of the authorities of the Catholic church.

The historical character of the church also represents that factor on the basis of which its origin and mystical 'utopia' must be conceived. So it is as a function of the real history of the churches that theological concepts must be constructed. The theologian will thus avoid the idealism towards which the temptation towards edification may exert pressure. History represents a principle of reality which is too rarely respected. So it is necessary to make its function in ecclesiology more precise.

3. The function of history in ecclesiology

The church is inseparable from its history. This too has a right of entry into theological reflection. That might appear self-evident, but it is something which was rarely recognized. As a social phenomenon Catholicism is little inclined to introduce history as an interpretative concept: the modernist crisis provides an example of the antipathy of the church authorities to this concept. In effect it puts in question the idea that a stable and invariable essence is maintained through modifications or mutations that may happen. The definition and control of this essence are assigned to indestructible church authorities. Now it has to be recognized that despite official and traditional reticence, history affects scripture, sacramentality, the councils, Christian customs, theological forms and church politics. None of these spheres in which there is Christian action and theory escaped a permanent transformation as a result of differentiated relations with other spheres. So the history of the churches is the factor on the basis of which it is in principle possible to talk of the church in a non-ideological way. In making this statement I am in no way excluding the privileged character of the New Testament and its critical power in respect of any later mutation. Two examples will illustrate my hypothesis: one is practical, Christian freedom in St Paul; the other dogmatic, the eschatological sanction.

1. Christian freedom is one of Paul's concerns. In Romans 6 he resumes the argument of Galatians and argues for a Christianity which is not a sorry repetition of the law but free action in the spirit. The gift of the spirit produces freedom.

Paul's proposals remain wishful thinking as long as they are not set over against the history of Christian groups. They have a different function once they are related to that history. At that point it must be honestly recognized:

(*a*) That in the short term Christian freedom did not play any part in questioning the existence of slavery in the Roman empire; that in the long term it had a certain effect, but not with any great force, since it was necessary to wait for abolitionism in the nineteenth century for an awareness of the full force of the contradiction between the affirmation of Christian freedom and social slavery. This observation shows how a view of Christian freedom would be idealistic and abstract if one failed to see how slow it was in producing social changes.

(*b*) That the affirmation of Christian freedom is not represented by the rights given to the subject, whether in the church or in society. Over the centuries, Christian freedom did not have any representation in the law: on the contrary, it served as an arsenal of repression, and provided the justification for a political and authoritarian church. People were freed by being made members of a church group. Only the Christian with the Spirit, i.e. the one who rightly belonged to the church, had the right to be a full citizen. The Inquisition was not a chance development, but embodied an effective concern to free those who were slaves or to render harmless to the group those who decided not to be converted. Catholicism had to wait for Vatican II to see the laws opposed to this secular practice given official approval. The Catholic church had to lose its dominant position for it to defend a right which was no longer regional or arbitrary, but unconditional.

So it is impossible to speak of Christian freedom without finding a place for what is said by the violent history of its emergence. Not to level any accusation but to cease to be idealistic. Outside its historical future freedom is not thought, but dreamed of. Outside effective and recognized law it can only be grasped as a cry or a revolt.[9]

2. The eschatological sanction. From the first centuries onwards, Christians have identified the church with the ark of salvation; they have considered baptism as the entry into this ark. It was only with Augustine, in the Pelagian dispute,[10] that what was involved in salvation was made more precise, notably in the case of small children. Without baptism, they were condemned to hell by reason of the gravity of Adam's sin. Infant baptism was also increasingly

28

associated with the need to snatch the infant from eternal death. One can measure the emotional concern expressed in this wish for baptism when one realizes the high level of infant mortality at the time. It was necessary to wait until the Middle Ages, and especially St Thomas, for Christians to envisage a less tragic fate for small children; they were no longer damned, i.e. they were not condemned to eternal suffering for a sin which was not their own. They were only condemned to being not as happy as they could have been: they were put in 'limbo', which gradually became the place of natural happiness. Recently, that is to say since the last world war, we have seen the abandonment of this view, which up to that point was widespread. The acceptance of Christian funeral rites for unbaptized infants is the sign of their being entrusted to the mercy of God, and therefore a sign of the present concern of Christians to say nothing specific about the fate of such children other than to express a hope for them. The most recent document on baptism[11] does not use the word 'limbo'; it refers to the entrusting of children to the divine mercy. Certainly there used to be theological attempts to think of other needs for baptism. However, the change has been brought about by the justified inability of the modern mind to accept collective sanctions: the infant is innocent of personal faults. The God who condemned such children would not be in accord with the God of the gospel, with the practical morality associated with the rights of man. Thus on a basic point of human destiny, a point which transforms earlier theories of sanctions and sin, the history of the church was an effective factor in bringing about change. Nothing seems to be irrevocably decided other than the involvement of God in our history in Jesus, but that is not represented by a rational and legal system the cultural and social effects of which we could deduce.

The two examples I have chosen relate to two different levels: one to Christian practice and the other to doctrine. Neither level escapes historical variation; the interplay in which meaning is expressed is not established once and for all, but does not cease to vary in relation to events, social systems, ideologies and cultures. So the church does not anticipate the kingdom of God as an ideal system of practice and doctrine. This kingdom in its historical phase is built up in a tentative way. I do not deny, though, that the churches have a structure, that is to say a logic of their interrelationship. This would be represented by the retention of differences in co-existence.

If there is any essence, it is the unifying energy of the relational system. The churches, too, have the unfolding of their history as a place of verification.

It is still necessary to specify what we mean by history. Two elements combine to fix the meaning of this term: a group tends to hold in its memory that which glorifies it, so history is celebration. Historical science tends to stress distance from the past, which is something that is lost.

A group remembers that which glorifies it: it writes the account of the main facts of its history. This is a selective memory. A study of biblical historiography already shows the point at which the reigns of David and Solomon were remembered as permanent models allowing all Hebrews to identify with the heroes who made the people great.[12]

The study of the Acts of the Apostles leads to identical remarks about the history of the primitive community: what is recalled is what glorifies it and allows identification with it as a transforming model. Perverse effects are eliminated.[13]

A study of the church history of Eusebius of Caesarea[14] leads to similar conclusions – and this is all the more interesting since Eusebius sees Constantine as the man who fulfils the ancestral dream of the church: unifying mysticism and politics, realizing the kingdom on earth.[15]

Hagiography prompts similar remarks: the processes of selection are also the processes of celebration.

In short, a society commemorates elements of its past to the degree to which this memory now allows it to distinguish itself in a worthy way from other societies and to imagine a future for itself.

This kind of memory in the churches partly hides the real movement in them by reducing their history to the drama of grace and sin. The needs of memory nourish a Manichaeism of individuals and events. Memory thereafter takes an apologetic form: it separates itself from effective history.

This aspect of 'celebration' affects the way in which church history is treated at the level of catechesis, preaching and official statements. These statements give the impression that the unity of faith and morality, the stability of the liturgy and the legal system, the persistence of a political line, justice and social function have been behind the churches from the beginning: thus such statements do away with effective history. There is then a scandal when this is discovered: the church was admired too much and the believer was too identified with history as celebration for him or her not to resent the divulgence of a less idyllic history as a snub. The passage from one writing of history to another proves a harsh test for faith.

In fact history, by its concern to reach a scientific level, parts company with the demands of the group. It acquires another status: it is not just chronicle and memory; it is not just narrative, but is a critical attempt to study the past as an object in the light of our present. Moreover its most tangible effect is to make us perceive the past as something that has been lost; it is always in the distance, impossible to restore. In this sense history demystifies celebration. The critical questioning of witnesses, the destructive effect that it can have on chronicles and narratives, the way in which it brings out gaps in our information, the attempt to define the actual sequences of cause and effect, restore to the past its somewhat precarious status: so the narrative will be demystified like the celebration it serves. Moreover, the work of criticism shows the impossiblity of restoring the past in its positive character. It has been lost; from now on it is a fact of language, subject to interpretation. This distancing frees the present from the past as a norm. There are societies which have succeeded in securing their future, but there are no model societies. The challenges to which ancient societies responded cannot be transposed to contemporary societies.

These thoughts about celebration and distancing have a particular application in ecclesiology. The church recalls its origin, it narrates it, not only in the case of Jesus but also in the case of the primitive community and the history of the chosen people. So the church is haunted by the memory of the supreme acts of God. The liturgy represents the ordinance which is celebrated. But the actualizing of this memory is a delicate operation: by their very structure, which is of their period, the biblical narratives and the accounts in the Gospels give the feeling of an immediacy of divine action in history. The theory of 'signs of the times' derives from a concern to discern in the present the main actions of God as actions which open up a future. In short, the liturgy is designed as a celebration both of a past history and of a history in the course of constructing itself.

On first acquaintance, the effect produced by scientific history was thought to be destructive. Then it was invoked to support the specifically Christian conviction that the God of Abraham and of Jesus is a God of history. However, the elimination of the aspect of 'celebration' led to more serious questions being asked about the introduction of scientific history into theology. In fact the abandonment of narrative had consequences for the interpretation of the effectiveness of the gospel.

A narrative presupposes actions to narrate, experiences to communicate, challenges to overcome. The biblical narratives, especially those of the books of Samuel and Kings, have things to talk about. The history of Eusebius of Caesarea also has something to talk about. But Eusebius ceases to have a story once Constantine makes Christianity the ideology of the empire: he writes as if history had stopped and the kingdom had come.[16] But history comes into its own again and the story regains its status because of the internal conflicts in the empire.[17] However, the narrative built up in this way presupposes, as in the mediaeval chronicles of the crusades, that the ecclesiastical narrator is convinced of writing history as God is directing it. The disappearance of narratives and chronicles from the modern European church bears witness to the feeling that the action of God in history is no longer easy to grasp. The quest for 'signs of the time' confirms this shift in conviction: the believer is no longer certain that membership of the church involves him in history written by God. Therefore he can no longer write the account. The Vatican II declaration 'The Church in the Modern World'[18] was not written as a narrative but developed in the form of an essay on certain problems. The church no longer celebrates its action in a narrative, as did the Hebrews, the primitive church and the mediaeval chronicles. Narratives indeed celebrate certain events: foundations of orders, biographies, pilgrimages and so on. But there are no longer global accounts. This disappearance of narrative can perhaps be related to the absence of the messianic hope, and consequently the disappearance of millenarianism. The efforts to restore a narrative vision to Christianity in Latin America and attempts at narrative theology[19] come up against the difficulty of collecting the material and constructing it as an 'epic'. So it is understandable that the actualization of the liturgy as a celebration of the mighty acts of God proves to be complex.

With the disappearance of narrative, scientific history takes a major place in the church. The more the church tends to be a celebration of its origin and the less it narrates its present action, the more necessary scientific study of its origin becomes. Justification is sought for the present penury of narrative as a result of the non-messianic situation of the church in the rejection of the original messianic qualities. In short, does not the demystification of narrative as celebration justify our inability to write such narrative in the present? Thus scientific history helps to relativize the energy of the group.

This desire, nowadays expressed by many Christians, to recreate effectively a history of liberation which can be a cause for celebration provides a proof in the other direction. Demystification leads to demobilization. Scientific history speaks of what is 'lost'; it lends plausibility to our inability to incorporate the freedom of the kingdom in the system of social relationships. The narrative counts on this capacity, since only effective capacity can be celebrated. However, we should add that the story is an object of celebration only once the action has been performed and thus lost. What is the object of celebration is also the object of scientific history. Hence narrative or scientific history are speaking of something that is lost. Only its action manifests the energy that is possible in the present. The narrative or the history are secondary; the action of history is primary: it corresponds to a praxis motivated by a utopia.

Thus reflection on the historicity of the church, simply because of the different ways of relating to it, leads us to ask what is the dynamic factor which has been behind the Christian group since its beginnings: utopia expressed in the imagery of the kingdom of God. This is not an ideal; it is implied in the way in which Christians relate to their own history. So it is part of a study of the church as it presents itself to us. 'Utopia' is inseparable from that which specifies it: faith in the coming of the kingdom. To be a believer is to have confidence in God about the coming of the kingdom and to join in forming a body (ecclesia) by reason of this confidence in the promise. That is the historical trace that we can find: it takes institutional form.

II

The Churches and the Institution

For about twenty years, particularly in France, it has been taken for granted that 'institution' is synonymous with 'repression'. To describe the church as institutional would seem more of a provocation or an archaism. However, in spite of the contemporary and specifically Christian antipathy to the institution, we must take account of the fact that the churches have survived the challenges of history at least in part by virtue of their institutional character. In fact they present themselves to us as associations with a precise aim, being endowed with a right to control relationships between their members, provided with means to realize their aim, and experienced by their members both as a possibility for development and as a constraint. It would, however, be frivolous to neglect contemporary opposition to institutions.

In fact the institution has taken on a pejorative colouring in recent debates.[1] The progressive wing of the Catholic church challenges its institutional aspect: it accuses it of being responsible for a decline in Christianity. Historically, the church as an institution is said to have preferred to ensure its survival rather than promote its mission. The task to be accomplished has hardly motivated its religious or political options: it has been more concerned to safeguard its privileges and its abstract universality. Thus the institution is often identified with 'bureaucracy, organization and centralization': in short, it is accused of making the church a 'cold monster' like the state. In our period of militancy in favour of personal, local, regional and cultural autonomy, the institutional character of the churches, notably of the Roman Catholic church, seems increasingly intolerable. Some see this institutional proliferation of the church of Rome as an obstacle to the proclamation of the gospel.

34

There is an explanation for these reactions of rejection: recent history, marked by an excess of Roman centralization and bureaucracy, though this was combatted by Vatican II, has heightened sensitivity towards all that is legalistic, objective, formal – in a word, institutional.

It is not for me to justify the church as an institution – that is a fact – but to demonstrate its function, significance and limits.

This concern governs the course we shall take. After a brief sociological description of the institution I shall look again at the institutional forms of the Roman church and end the chapter with what seems to me to be the underlying factor in all Christian questions about the church as an institution: the tension between a hierarchical system and the great biblical images focussed on the notion of a people.

1. The institution, a brief description

The aim of this brief description is to shed light on those difficulties presented by the church as an institution which relate to its historicity. An institution is not a Platonic ideal.

My starting point is the definition given by P.Robert in his *Dictionnaire alphabétique et analogique de la langue française* (*Petit Robert*, Paris 1967, 918):

> *Institution*… 3 The thing instituted (person, morality, group, reǵime)… Absolute. The institutions, the totality of social forms or structures as they are established by law or custom, and especially those which derive from public law.

If this definition is right, an institution can be recognized by its constraining character. The constraint is not univocal, but there are degrees to it: politeness does not have the same constraints as fiscal laws. Without constraint an institution would disappear. So the problem comes down to determining the effectiveness of the constraint.

In the *Encyclopedia Universalis* (Paris 1968, 8, s.v. 'Institutions', 1062-5), F.Bourricaud relates the institution to a force, an authority. Both force and morality rest on a moral foundation. The constraint is not the force, which appears only in the case of deviation: penal law is secondary to the laws defining the rules of the social game.

The moral foundation of the institution is based on two factors: respect (engendering legitimacy) and autonomy.

First, respect, by which I understand taking seriously the obligations imposed by the institution. Once an institution ceases to be respectable and credible, whether because its rules are anachronistic or it is simply camouflage for private interests (one might think of the criticism of capitalism and the state in Marx or the concept of the class struggle which defines as formal the bourgeois law with its universal claims), it will either be no longer effective or will seek to prolong its ancient legitimation by force.

Two conditions ensure the respectability or legitimacy of an institution.

One condition is a living link between beliefs and the institution. A crisis of belief over the ends or means of an institution robs it of its legitimacy. At the very least it means that it is no longer self-evident. In the modern period, when knowledge is widely spread through the population, the mere fact of having an authoritative role is no longer enough to make credible decisions which affect all the subjects of an institution.

The other condition is an obvious fairness between the contributions required by the institution, that is to say the burdens imposed on the individual to assure its functioning, and its rewards, its beneficial aspect.

Thus in societies with democratic beliefs, the Roman church loses credibility as a result of its requirement that laity shall be devoted to its cause without any effective power sharing, i.e. its treatment of them as subjects.

In short, the constraints of an institution are accepted only if there is an effective consensus over its explicit aims.

The second factor which forms the moral foundation of an institution is autonomy. This condition is only apparently in opposition to a recognition of the constraints imposed by institutions.

Here the term 'autonomy' takes on a precise significance: it signifies that the individual is not the author of institutional constraints; they precede him and do not define him. By education which engenders conviction he internalizes them, because he recognizes that they are working in favour of his personal development. So the constraints are effective if they are internalized by a process

36

of socialization. But the individual only internalizes them if they give him or her some chance of development.

For either they express the necessary consent of the individual to the functioning of institutions, of society, by allowing him or her to participate happily in them, or they are alien to the individual: the institution, in that case using force or violence to perpetuate itself, loses its legitimacy. So one ends up with a state of lawlessness, since individuals are left to their desires and interests. The institutional order weakens at the same time as autonomy perishes.[2] In short the institution can impose constraints only if they are felt to be beneficial by individuals.

2. The institutional forms of the church

In an article entitled 'The Development of the Church as Subject: An Aspect of Vatican II',[3] H.Legrand uses the term 'church as subject' for the local church in order to avoid using the term 'community' too often as a designation of the church. He justifies his mistrust of this description in this way: it seems to him illegitimate to deduce the relevance of a concept for describing the *de facto* functioning of the Roman church from its dogmatic validity. A number of sociologists have drawn the attention of theologians to the problems of an indiscriminate use of this term. In fact the study of community movements in Europe shows that this is to exalt a single form of belonging to the church, one in which personal and direct relationships are dominant – something which presupposes broad areas of common cultural interests and elective affinities. In short this is to set up a kind of sociality in a model form without noting that in an operation of this kind there are exclusions which arise because the basic social data are unconsciously governed by a particular cultural ethos and not by the demands which arise from the gospel.

Finally Legrand indicates that this stress on a line in which only interpersonal relationships predominate is furthered by the *de facto* break between theological language and canonical language. Ecclesiologists have underestimated the importance of canon law for their discipline, and the word 'legalistic' has become pejorative. Thus it has been belatedly discovered that conciliar texts pass into the life of the Roman church through the mediation of law. So anyone wanting to talk about the church must not ignore the institutional problem.

To show the significance of this, I shall refer to a text of Vatican II, which will offer a starting point for our reflections.

In the Constitution on the Liturgy, no.41,[4] we are told that the local church is the supreme manifestation of the church of God because it is brought into being in the liturgical assembly and especially in eucharistic celebration.

The conciliar text is concerned with a manifestation, i.e. with a visible form. It does not describe an informal association but a sacramental celebration in which the roles are not interchangeable. It is about a local church which realizes in that place the universal church of God. That signifies at least that the people assembled here is the church, that it is not part of a whole the centre of which is elsewhere. The whole is present here, in this manifestation.

This conciliar presentation of the visible church is very different from that which we read in a work by R.Bellarmine:

The one true church is the community of men assembled by the profession of the same Christian faith, communicating the same sacraments, under the government of legitimate pastors, and especially of the one vicar of Christ on earth, the Roman pontiff.[5]

According to Bellarmine three criteria determine the church: the profession of the true faith, communion in the same sacraments and submission to legitimate pastors.

These three criteria are determined by the central government, the Roman pontiff. They allow the exclusion from the church of all those who do not correspond to these visible criteria of which the central government is the author.

A comparison of these two presentations shows that there are different ways of taking account of the institutional character of the church.

In the first case it is defined in terms of local celebration. It is a matter of 'institutionality', since according to the text the church *qua* sacrament precedes the assembly: in sociological terms it is a constraint.

In the second case, by contrast, the institutional character of the church is denoted by the legitimating criterion of the government, a criterion which redefines the other elements: the 'institutionality' is thus manifested at the level of the authorities.

The difference between the second case and the first explains the construction of the constitution *Lumen Gentium*:[6] this sought to avoid making the church an institution the sole criteria of which would be the legitimacy of the government or the authorities. Moreover it is only after having spoken of the people of God that the constitution reviews elements which organize it in structural terms.

The designation 'people of God' is ambiguous. Let me explain what Vatican II means by the expression before putting forward its structural elements.

According to Vatican II believers form the people of God. As a result every local church is the people of God. It is not less than the universal church. All are equal: 'there is no longer Jew nor Greek... man nor woman...' There is one person in Jesus Christ. The differentiations which emerge in the structuring of this people are secondary: they do not extend to primary rights. The Catholic church does not represent a pyramidal system or a descending series of intermediaries: God, Jesus Christ, the Pope, the bishops, the priests, the lay people. However, this theological perspective remains wishful thinking or an ideology if the effective institutional and legal structures do not specifically honour the theory that the church is none other than the people called together by God, assigning to all equality and freedom in Christ.[7] Vatican II defines the basis of this law by the concept of 'common priesthood' on which the charisms are grafted.[8]

The church is a people; it is not a mob, a mass or an aggregate of individuals.

This conviction is already present in the belief that the church is anticipated by the chosen people: the destiny of the Jewish people mediates that of the individual; the vocation of the Jewish people defines that of the individual. So to say that the church is the people of God amounts to affirming that the people, founded on the divine calling of an eschatological vocation, precedes all individuality and every individual vocation. In classical terms, the individual relationship to God is not primary, independently of all socialization: the divine calling is aimed at constituting humanity as a people by reason of its common eschatological destiny.

The difficulty posed by these affirmations does not arise at the level of the indication of universalism: the priority of the people over the individual by reason of its one eschatological destiny; it appears in the institutional treatment of this affirmation. As soon as the notion of people of God ceases to be ideal or vague, as soon as it institutionalizes or historicizes itself, how are the rights of the people articulated by reason of its calling and what expression is given to those of the individual? How is the work of socialization to be accomplished with the aim of 'subjecting' the individual to the goals of the people? The treatment of these problems calls for reflection on the institution: the people is not an 'ideality'; it is historical.

The people of God is historical: the text of *Lumen Gentium*[9] says so. According to this text the people begins with Abel and will go on growing to the end of history. It is in this vast fresco that the conciliar constitution puts the church as people. So this is certainly not an ideal people: one cannot define it simply in terms of an inner call from God. In that case one would have a juxtaposition of individual believers and not a people. So it is necessary to indicate what criteria make talk of a people possible. The conciliar text uses two of them: the first Mosaic covenant which gave birth to the Hebrew people and the second covenant which gave birth to the church.[10]

These two criteria posit the obvious link between the people constituted and instituted in this way and the *ex hypothesi* universality of the calling. The constitution itself indicates how difficult these questions are.[11]

To recapitulate the Council's view briefly: the people of God is a people formed by the divine call, signifying the unity of an eschatological destiny, the kingdom. The condition of this people is the dignity and freedom of the sons of God, so all have equal rights. It is the church, although all those who are not members of the visible churches are not excluded from it.

Thus the centre around which the presentation of the church in *Lumen Gentium* is organized is the category of the people of God. This makes it possible at the same time neither to reduce the mystical vision – this is not just any people, but that which God has called for his kingdom – nor to leave out the institution: a people is structured; it is not an agglomeration of individuals. St Thomas defined the church as *congregatio fidelium* (the assembly of the faithful). This institutional aspect of the people is the one which is the object of history, and at the same time is its subject. To be the subject of history is to introduce transformations into its very structure. From this perspective Vatican II marks a mutation of thought about the institutions of the church. To make this clear I shall contrast it with the notion of the church which emerged from the Counter-Reformation.

The church which emerged from the Counter-Reformation in the rush of decisions made by the Council of Trent (1545-1563) is the result of polemic and differentiation.

The churches of the Reformation essentially wanted to hand the church over to believers and broke with the earlier system on two points: they abolished the distinction between priestly ministry and common ministry, and they rejected the domination of Rome.

The Catholic church which emerged from the Counter-Reformation stressed the power of the ordained ministry and the pre-eminence of Rome. So it ended up with the image of a church organized around the Roman Pontiff of whom the bishops in each diocese were the prefects. The priests were the local delegates of the latter, with the aim of governing the Christian people for its good.

This kind of organization was called pyramidal.

There were two ideological justifications for it: the first was infallibility, and the second was the christological supremacy which excluded the role of the Spirit.

Infallibility was not directly a matter of the dogmatic pronouncement, which is sober and negative, but of its usage or social function. It served to give Rome a pre-eminence over the dispersed episcopacy; it made the episcopacy cease to be of any importance in the government of the church, each bishop being personally in relationship with Rome, but having no relations with his colleagues. There was talk of 'vertical relations' without 'horizontal relations' between them.

As for christological pre-eminence, the Pope is the vicar of Christ; he is his representative in the world. In the midst of the challenges of history he expresses the continuity of the action of Christ. By reason of this pre-eminence, the gift of the Spirit made to the church, which is so important in Orthodoxy, is reduced to the internalization of what is otherwise proclaimed at the supreme summit of the hierarchy.

The legal consequences are evident: the multiplicity of powers exercised in the church is in effect dependent on Rome, whether these are in the sphere of everyday discipline, like marriage or liturgy, or in the framework of reflection (the Congregation for the Doctrine of Faith) or action.

The autonomy recognized in the dioceses and regions is parsimonious. The churches linked with Rome which have their own tradition are deprived of the right to found missions in conformity with their rite (the Greek church, Maronite church, etc.); only the law of the Roman church has universal validity. As a result, Catholic believers are invited to think, pray and organize themselves according to identical norms in Rome, Lima or Tokyo.

In theory Vatican II broke this pyramidal organization by instituting new relational structures in the Roman church. I list some of them here:

A permanent link has been created between the Roman primacy and the episcopal college. The aim of this legal structure is evident: to restore real power to the bishops as a body in the church and as a result no longer to limit their role to that of prefects or delegates of the central government.

From now on the bishops are the effective representatives of the local churches over whose destinies they preside. The latter are whole churches and not a department of the Roman church, of which Rome would be the centre. The episcopal colleges do not do away with the primacy of the Bishop of Rome; they deny him the privilege of being comparable to the central government of nations.

The link between the Roman primacy and the episcopal college takes specific form in the institution of synods summoned by bishops, in the reform of the Roman curia,[12] and in the establishment of permanent episcopal assemblies at a regional, national and international level.

In this reordering of relations between the bishops and Rome, two trends represent a marked break with the policy of the preceding period: the role given to the local churches, in particular by the institution of synods; and the stress on a pastoral and doctrinal unity of the episcopate of a region or nation.

Here are some elements which make these trends quite clear.

1. The creation of an organic link within the local church between the bishop, the priests and the laity. This link is expressed in a twofold institution:

(*a*) That of the 'presbyterium', the aim of which was to break the isolation of secular priests and make them participate in the episcopal power of decision.

(*b*) That of the 'pastoral council', encouraging chosen laity to participate in the bishop's government. This is seen as a way of abolishing the dependence of the laity on the clergy and making the church their church.

2. Encouragement to promote new forms of ministry: this point has proved more delicate. Experience after the Council bears witness to the involvement of laity in catechesis, and the introduction of lay presidents (men or women) of communities to take the place of priests. So far there has been no legally formulated expression of this major movement in which laity have taken over work in the church and only the diaconate has enjoyed this privilege because it is an ancient institution.

3. The appearance of basic communities, often officially inserted into the fabric of the institutional church, as in certain Latin American countries. These have gradually transformed the traditional role of the parishes.

These comments have been brief. The institutional renewal which is emerging in the Catholic church really calls for a thorough study of the new Code of Canon Law and a list of new practices and their institutional effects. One could then ask whether the pyramidal system set up after the Reformation has actually been shaken, and whether this has opened up the way for another type of ecclesiology, with some hope of a reply.

By way of a test I have chosen three revived institutions: the Roman synods, the national councils of bishops, and the local assemblies round the bishop. An examination of the way in which they function should allow us to assess whether or not Vatican II did indeed launch a transformation in the direction of democracy.

1. The international Roman synods represent a novelty in the government of the church. They express its diversity. But has the way they have in fact worked out lived up to the hopes set on them for a decentralization of the church? Are the bishops themselves

self-censored, so as not to go against the views of the Pope? What I mean is, have they spoken according to what the Pope is supposed to want or according to the experiences of their respective churches? Have they formed an intermediary group or an oligarchy?[13] Or have they played a sort of democratic game?

2. The national councils of bishops have aroused great hopes for the politics and pastoral work of a local church. But are they the place where the problems of a federation of local churches are discussed openly from the point of view of information? Or are these assemblies the place where a new bureaucracy is produced which paralyses the local bishop and sterilizes the assembly? The functioning of such assemblies is still too recent for us to be able to give an honest reply to these questions. However, they are worth raising since they are based on the indication of real tensions.

3. Finally, at the level of the local church, have the presbyterium and the pastoral council been the places where power has truly been shared? In particular, do the laity always have the feeling of not being heard and having no part in decisions? If that is the case, is this feeling well-founded or imaginary?

In the present state of our information let us recognize that:

1. The transition from a pyramidal image of the church to a disseminated power has led to a change in sensitivity the perceptible effects of which have been judged to be indications of crisis: statements, discussions, informal groups, liturgical creativity, bold political commitment, liberties with official rules about marriage, the decline in the credibility of the Curia, irritation at interventions by Rome. Every society in the process of liberalization goes through a period of anomia.

2. The transition from a pyramidal image to that of a disseminated power has so far not been accompanied by a law which safeguards the internal relationships of these institutions and their internal functioning.

The promulgation of the new Code of Canon Law is too recent to allow us to get a clear idea on this point. However, the first commentaries[14] lead us to understand that its structure does not completely reflect the changes which took place at Vatican II; the law marks a retreat from the ideas which were expressed in theory at the Council. So there is a discrepancy between the promises made at the Council and the application of its decrees. The weaknesses in the law perceived after the Council remain. They have played a part and still play a part:

1. In a return to the procedures inherent in the old image, that is, specifically in the interventions of Rome which effectively limit the power of the local churches, whether this power is legitimate or not. The power of these churches has not been laid down anywhere, and that explains why the national synods have often been held amid feelings of frustration, their proposals having been reduced to wishful thinking. That could have serious consequences for the credibility of the institution, as I indicated when discussing the acceptance of constraint.[15] This return to former practices is reinforced by the media. Only the voice of the Pope is heard – all the more so since he travels. The local churches are reduced to silence.

2. In the excessively informal character of the decision-making authorities, synods and assemblies. This risks giving the effective power to a permanent bureaucracy.

At the end of this very rapid review of institutional trends which arose out of Vatican II I can see a lack of theological reflection on the functioning of the Catholic church: there has been much celebration of the new ecclesiology of Vatican II but little account has been taken of the discrepancy between the ideal, the law and its application. I personally think it essential for ecclesiology to include reflection on the distance between the idea of the church as promulgated in scripture or at the Council and its transcription into tangible functioning.

So it would be of some interest to bring out the reasons why the Roman primacy tends to be represented in specific terms by centralization and the obliteration of the local churches as partners in dialogue, which are not just socio-cultural and political, but equally ideological or doctrinal: the current resumption of the debate on infallibility, on *receptio*,[16] is not prompted by dogmatic difficulties but by the perverse effects of the way in which the institution functions. If there are dogmatic difficulties, they will have come out of the specific consequences of Vatican II and not out of the decision itself.

That makes me regret that contemporary ecclesiology should be concentrated more on biblical images (body of Christ, bride, etc.)

that on institutionality. Having said that, I am not in any way praising the institutional ecclesiology of the Counter-Reformation. On the contrary, I am against its lack of critical reflection on the institution because it sacralized it. It made the discrepancy between utopia and the institution quite insignificant. However, it is precisely this distance that we have to think about. The monopoly now accorded to images or eschatology relieves us of thinking about it, just as the sacralization of the institution did previously. The historical institution of the church (that is to say, the institution in evolution) is at the same time both an active subject and the object of reflection. The changes desired and sketched out in so many areas by Vatican II, but not taken up in law or incorporated into theology (there has been hardly any ecclesiology since Vatican II), bear witness to the need to articulate in thought about the church the promise of the kingdom which it confesses and the provisional character which it represents in institutional form.

3. The institutional question: the hierarchical system and biblical images

Vatican II discussed the hierarchical constitution of the church in *Lumen Gentium*, ch.III, after its exposition of the people of God and the mystery of the church. Some people have wanted to see this progression from the invisible mystery to the structuring of the people of God in a visible society as an inversion of the theology of the church dominant in the nineteenth century, a theology which was then organized around a purely hierarchical reflection, a theology of powers. Vatican II, by stating in *Lumen Gentium*, paragraph 18, that those who hold a 'sacred' power in the Catholic church, notably the Bishop of Rome and all the bishops, hold it in the service of the people of God, is said to have wanted to show that the hierarchical structure of the church only made sense in relation to the growth and unity of this people. The primary factor is the people on the way to the kingdom. The spiritual power is made for the people, not the people for the spiritual power. However, difficulties remain: in part they are associated with the use of biblical images and in part with the way in which the hierarchy is presented. After indicating the difficulties inherent in Vatican II, I shall consider the institutional problem in a more radical way.

Difficulties inherent in Vatican II

The hierarchical model which was put forward by the ecclesiology dominant in the nineteenth century has attracted justified criticism: in it the church was in effect defined in terms of the episcopal body and papal power. For their own good, the role of the laity was to carry out decisions which emanated from their pastors: in other words, they were dependent subjects.

Vatican II is meant to have remedied this situation of dependence, socially indefensible because it breaks with modern ideas and responsibilities. Recalling the original intent of the church, the free calling by God in Jesus brought about through the gift of the Spirit and leading to the *absolute equality* of all before God (cf.§32), the Council was thought to have broken with the inegalitarian and antidemocratic ideology of the earlier ecclesiology. This opinion seems to me to be too optimistic. In fact the call to the original intent of the church has been relativized by two elements: the biblical imagery and the place of the laity.

First the biblical images (§6): sheepfold, flock, field, vine, God's building, holy temple, holy city, betrothed, body of Christ.

All the images have God, Christ or the Spirit as active subjects. God is the shepherd, the farmer, the vine-tender, the builder, the heart of the temple, the head of the city, the husband, the life of the mystical body. When used in connection with God or the Spirit or even of the risen Christ, these images, which are all passive ones (the action goes only in one direction), *ex hypothesi* do not cause any difficulty: the active subject is not institutionalized and therefore socialized, since essentially he is invisible: he is the Wholly Other, by reason of his absence from the field of experience.

The function of these biblical images changes once the organizing idea of ch.III, the hierarchical constitution of the church, appears. God, Christ or the Spirit are only the active subjects on the basis of their absence from experience or society; the active subjects are the bishops assisted by the priests (§21) who make Jesus Christ present in the midst of believers: thus the one who is absent in human terms becomes the one who is made present through the hierarchical body. In ecclesiology inspired by the Reformation the one who is absent is made present by the one Word to whom classically the sacrament is assimilated (§21). The resumption of the images of §6 has institutional consequences, i.e. consquences which can be detected on the level of social constraint. These consequences are evident in ch.IV, which is devoted to the laity. There we read that their vocation is the conduct of temporal matters which they order in accordance with God's will, but not the government of the church; the hierarchical body allows them to show their feelings, hears their advice and lets them enjoy a certain freedom of action, but all this happens as if the passsive metaphors taken from the Bible defined the line of interpretation of their situation in the Catholic church (§37).

This raises the problem of the institution: on the one hand, no inequality can be allowed in the church which derives from race, nation, social condition or sex; on the other hand a hierarchical constitution only allows the laity a narrow participation in the internal government of the church which is constantly a matter of concession. In theory, dignity and equality are proclaimed, but in practice submission is required. Besides, this is the way in which the problem is seen in practice by active Catholic believers. This discrepancy leads to disagreement.

The discrepancy becomes manifest in the lack of connection between:

On the one hand the description of the people of God within whom the Spirit raises up ministries and charisms;

On the other hand, the hierarchical constitution which emerges from the choice of the apostles and is transmitted by tradition without any apparent connection with the first description.

Thus we end up with two parallel elements: the people who are called and their ministers. These two elements are harmonized both through their common origin (the will of God in Christ) and through a moral articulation, service. But the togetherness of the people and the hierarchy is presented as a positive datum of scripture without being thought of in terms of the institutionalism needed for the journey of the people towards its goal.

These parallel facts of the gathering of the people and the institution of the hierarchical body are radically unified in the following postulate:

By reason of the will of Christ who calls them into being and institutes them, there can be no opposition between them since the object of the life of the people is the revealed mystery and the object

48

of the teaching, worship and government by the hierarchy is this same mystery, the limits of hierarchical power being the limits of revelation. The concept of functional infallibility is the specific sign of this harmony: the Pope and the episcopacy, making use of their supreme authority, can only utter the revelation which by the gift of the Spirit animates the life of the people. In short, the hierarchical body expresses in rigorous language the theological experience of believers. No opposition is possible *a priori*, since the unity is given by the terms Christ or the Spirit.

This internal harmony with an institutional effect explains:

The use of a moral category like that of service: it seeks to exorcize the idea of power and domination which history risks evoking.

The idyllic description given of the hierarchical ministry by *Lumen Gentium*.

The call to obey the hierarchy, a call based on assistance from the Spirit.

Forgetfulness of the harsh historical conflicts within the church between movements emerging from the grass roots and the hierarchy.

In the course taken by Vatican II the conflicts are the effects of sin: they do not derive from the discrepancy between the interests of the Christian people, which may well be based on the gospel, and the hierarchical institutions which can no longer appear to serve them. The fact that this aspect has been hidden shows that the institutional problem remains distressing for the Catholic church.

Lumen Gentium did not think of the distance between the avowed aims of the organization and its weight, which simultaneously puts a strain on every institution and makes the development possible. For *Lumen Gentium*, in effect the constraint disappears, as a result of pre-established harmony. Obedience is presented in it as the freedom of the children of God (§37). Autonomy is acquired without conflict through internalization due to the gift of the Spirit.

The transformations longed for and the developments desired have no justifiable foundation since there is accord between the life of the people and the action of the hierarchy by reason of their original unity. Moreover all distance slides over into the order of sin. In spite of the affirmation that the people of God is historical we are dealing with an external history: the church, for all that it is faithful to its own origins, has no history; its institutionality is given

49

as the architecture of a perfect society. The theology of the Counter-Reformation is not dead. The basic concept of this theology, that of the perfect society, is still at work. The emergence of the dispute after Vatican II was already built into the contradictions between its proclamations and the development of a theology of compromise which finally left the hierarchy dominant. The conflict between John Paul II and the church in Nicaragua is a recent example.[17]

The institutional problem in the Catholic church

The harmony put forward by Vatican II between the aims of the ecclesiastical hierarchy in church government (i.e. those of the Catholic episcopacy in communion with the Pope) and the aspirations of the Christian people is an ideal one: it comes up against a double challenge, that of memory and that of present experience.

First that of memory: the history of the church is not an idyllic history. Neither the hierarchy nor the Christian people can generally lay claim to a constant harmony between their aims and aspirations and the demands of the gospel. Neither the one nor the other can guarantee that there has always been a healthy judgment about the *de facto* situation of the church and the decisions that have to be taken. The two have often pursued opposed interests, sometimes in the conviction of working for the gospel. The latent anticlericalism, particularly in France, is a good example of this failure to function. Proclaiming harmony leads to blotting out the mistakes of history. So one is led to a celebration of history the aim of which is to ensure peace in the present.

Then there is the challenge of present experience: the two decades which have elapsed since Vatican II have demonstrated that the harmony between the hierarchy and the people is not a datum, but can only be the result of a compromise and is always provisional. The conflicts inherent in the churches of Latin America, Holland and France, conflicts which emerged from opposed judgments on the role of Rome in the respective situations of these churches, cannot be resolved by appeal to this harmony. The risk is that they may be resolved by the domination of a tendency supported by the power of the hierarchy. Vatican II wanted to avoid this system of constraint.

In reality, at the heart of this clash between the harmony that is said to exist and memory or present experience is the institution: it is constraint supported to the degree that it accords or promises the expected benefits. Harmony is here put at such a level, namely that of mystical grandeur or the end of history in brotherhood and sisterhood, that it cannot provide proofs of its correctness. It is also necessary for there to be institutional anticipations of the aim represented by harmony, otherwise the conflict can deteriorate to the point of a break. I have chosen two current indications of the demands of the institution which are opposed to the ideology of pre-established harmony: ministry and the function of the papacy.

1. Ministry: the question is a tricky one and I have no intention of making an exhaustive study of it. It should be enough to say that the reflections offered here are organized around the appropriation of the Catholic church by all the major interests.

Vatican II proclaimed that the church is a people. A people is not a disorganized crowd, subject to the contradictions of drives and demagogues. A people is structured; it is in the hands of authorities to direct and control its present and its future. Ministry has its role in this function of guidance. But guidance is not the same thing as appropriation. That is why Vatican II thought to put a check on the idea of power with that of service. The check remains ideal if it is only moral: it has to have an institutional base. Now the way of thinking about and organizing ministry in the Catholic church tends to make institutional control useless, and the endorsement of moral control hides the lack of any effective control. Let me make this point more specific, since it is important for the institutional question.

The ministry exists for people. That would be a succinct summary of the formal structure of *Lumen Gentium*, inserting the hierarchy into the people of God and putting it at the service of this people. But this ministry does not hold its 'power' from the people; it receives it from Christ. We can understand this conviction if we recall the church's vocation, which is to live from the Spirit. Nothing gives the Spirit but Christ: the people receives the Spirit, and those who are in the service of the people receive this 'charism' from the Spirit so that they can live by the Spirit.[18]

Unfortunately, from this fundamental fact about the ministry is deduced an institutional organization which deprives those who are also the church, the laity, of a role in governing the church. The ministry in its 'sacramental' or 'spiritual' structure is one thing: the institutional organization of the church which must do justice to all those who have an interest in living from the Spirit and translating it into 'social' terms is another. The fact that 'all authority comes from God' does not say anything specific about the political form of the organization of a people or about the way in which its authorities are designated. This Pauline principle[19] affirms that all authorities are under the judgment of God and are not the masters of good and evil. That the ministry is a charism does not prejudge the way in which it is regulated and controlled within the Christian people. Now with the concept of pre-established harmony, everything happens as if social control were useless: the ministry includes the organization of the government. As a result lay Christians think that they have no part in the decisions which concern them. The dispute in the Catholic church is fuelled by this banishment of the laity from the level of decision-making authorities.

This feeling is reinforced by the legal elements which restrict access to the ministry: the need to be masculine and celibate. I am not certain that the authorities of the Catholic church have assessed the effects of recent documents on this matter.[20] Contrary to what has been said in some contexts,[21] the problem is not that of a right to the ministerial 'charisma' bound up with the sacrament. It is of a right of every Christian to have responsibility in the church. No one denies this right, and the bishops themselves have issued a call to exercise it effectively.[22] But there is an institutional contradiction between this call, based on the radical worth of all in the Spirit, and the barrier raised against sharing in the development of decisions by the need to belong to a 'clerical order', access to which is legally closed to some. Thus half of Christians, women, have no right to participate in the government of the church: they are banished from 'power' by their incapacity to be ministers on grounds of their sex. It is not so much the refusal to confer 'priesthood' on them which is difficult to take but the fact that this refusal bars them from all real social participation in church decisions. The same argument goes for the exclusion of married people. Women in general and married men can be consulted, but cannot take part in government.

So if the question of ministry needs to be rethought, it is not only because of the numerical lack of clergy or the scandal of churches without a minister, but primarily because it is an odious practice, at a time when the church is congratulating itself on working at the effective sharing of power in civil society, to exclude *a priori* a majority of Christians from the government of the church. This organization of the government of the institution appears to be a constraint not matched by real benefits. It remains suspect, at the level of government, of pursuing interests which are not those of the people of God. The confiscation of major decisions by the Roman authority reinforces this feeling of frustration.

2. The second instance of the clash between the institution and the idea of pre-established harmony is the function of the Pope. The journeys of John-Paul II have drawn attention to the exercising of ministry by the Bishop of Rome. To begin with, these journeys raised great hopes: by leaving Rome the Pope would meet Christians of other churches. Many expected a relaxation of Roman politics as a result: its diversification, the ultimate abandonment of unity in the cultural mode of a church. However, despite some positive contributions, the style imposed on the Pope's journeys by diplomatic necessities, the imperatives of security, the compulsive sensationalizing by the mass media, have orientated them on an unhealthy form of universality. The meetings in fact have remained formal: the assembled crowds do not allow any other relationship than that of the messenger to those whom he comes to teach. The episodes of the intervention of an American sister arguing the cause of women and of the celebration in Managua[23] bear witness to the artificial character of the encounter. More serious, though, is the fact that the mass media are gradually forcing John-Paul II to be seen as the episcopal authority of the Catholic church, the bishops being reduced by the very business of representation to the role of assistants or prefects. Which leads me to wonder whether this excess, which is duly deplored, is simply the result of external constraint or whether it comes from the majority understanding of the papacy in Catholicism.

I personally think that it would be hypocritical to attribute the hypertrophy of the function of the Pope only to external constraints: it is rooted in a secular usage falsely based on a decision which is said to be dogmatic: that of Vatican I on papal infallibility.[24]

This decision is rarely studied by itself; light is rarely shed on the restrictions which go with it and people stick to the level of the symbolic connotation which determines its usage.[25]

The decision expresses a conviction about the authority for church unity, the Bishop of Rome, which applies to all the church: the Spirit preserves it from failing in respect of the truth of the gospel in the face of challenges which are vital for its future. By his function, and as a representative of the faith of the church which he expresses, the Pope is given the negative guarantee that he will not put forward as a demand of the gospel anything that does not correspond to the desire of the Spirit animating all the church. But the more the conviction can be shared, the more the use that has been and is made of it can be disputed.

It can be disputed primarily by virtue of the inadmissible shift from the authority of certain functional acts to the person of the Pope. The latter is not infallible: such an infallibility would have no meaning and is invalidated by the history of the church. Some decisions taken in the name of all the church in connection with challenges vital to the faith can be infallible. They are necessarily very rare, and they do not in any way enhance the person of the Pope; they bear witness to the support of the church by the Spirit. The person of the Pope remains what it is: brilliant or mediocre, authoritarian or democratic, inspired by the gospel or thirsty for power. He is like any other being, human or Christian. To move from the idea of the infallibility of legally controlled decisions to the person is to rob the other institutional authorities in the church of all their value.

The usage of this conviction can also be disputed: the cult of the personality of the Pope which stems from the mystical drift of infallibility exaggerates the ministerial function of the unity of the church. It leads to a depreciation of the other functions of his presidency and authority in the church and does not leave them more space for the freedom which is needed for real links with the grass roots.

Thus the hypertrophy of the function of the Pope gets in the way of coping with the institutional problem in the church: faced with the problems posed by the basic communities in South America and in Europe, faced with decisions to be taken to alleviate the numerical shortfall in the ministry, faced with the need to reunite the diocesan or national synods without disappointing the particpants, faced with the proliferation of Roman documents on the most varied subjects, faced with the unilateral decisions of Rome on everyday morality, the local, regional, national or continental authorities are helpless.

I do not think that it is laid down that part of the practice of the ministry of unity should be to scorn other authorities. Neither the institutional problem of the Catholic church which Vatican II had hoped to cope with by the creation of collegiality nor the organic link with the other churches will find a solution as long as the Pope performs his role in such a way as to pay homage to the symbolic connotation of the holy and infallible leader. It is necessary for the function of unity again to become one ministry among others and not the sole ministry; that is to say, it should be in conformity to the plan suggested by Vatican II. Unfortunately this plan was too idealistic. Can such a characteristic be avoided by an institution which claims to administer the gift of the Spirit? I want to end this chapter by looking at this question: it will lead us towards the provisional status of the historical church.

The institutional administration of 'grace'

A Polish author, L.Kolakowski, has written a substantial work entitled *Christians without Churches* (Paris 1970). I mention it because it discusses anti-institutional mystical movements in the Protestant and Catholic churches of the seventeenth century. I shall not go into the details of the analyses produced by the author, but just mention his theory, which is relevant to the problem with which we are concerned here.

Kolakowski has noted in the mystical movements of the seventeenth century an antipathy, if not a repugnance, to the church as an institution: they regarded it as an intrusion into the process of access to God. In these movements it was thought that this access had to be opened up from God himself, and so could not be measured by anything other than the gift of the Spirit. The mixing of external elements with the dynamism of the mystical relationship could only be damaging. The gift of the Spirit is not of itself linked with any institution. These movements affirmed that they had no need either of hierarchical organizations or of the sacramental support of the churches. Kolakowski thinks that it is legitimate to present the problem of these mystics in this way: how can one imagine a spiritual gift as being subject to the authority of an institutional function? In fact, in their view hierarchical authority would disappear in favour of the spiritual man. Nothing would 'mediate' the union of God in the Spirit: this gives direct access to the freedom of the children of

God. So where the Spirit is left free to act, the institutional church no longer has a *raison d'être*. But in that case is it not contradictory for the churches to want to point the way to God, since the success of their concern involves their disappearance?

Kolakowski thinks that he can discover an explanation in Christianity itself for this contradiction in the politics of the historical churches, which engender within themselves a desire for the disappearance of their institutional character. Christianity is the vehicle for a unifying concept: grace as the absence of order. On the basis of this concept Kolakowski develops the following hypothesis:

The God of the New Testament is an innovator in comparison with the God of the Old Testament: he is no longer a legislator but a very intimate father. He pardons because he does not judge according to the law, requiring compensation, but loves human beings as his children. And in return human beings love him because he has made them exist as his children: they no longer fear him. So in religion we end up with the replacement of the order of law with an irrational family bond. This marks the summit of the Christian vision of the world. One can certainly produce a theological reconciliation of the figures of the lawgiver and the father with the use of psychoanalytical patterns. This attempt at speculation does not have any specific representation in Christian life because the two images call for attitudes which do not fit. It is illusory to want to live them both out simultaneously. In fact they are mutually exclusive, since either we obey the commandments out of fear and are in the realm of the law or we submit to them out of disinterested love, and enter into the perspective of the gospel.

This second attitude gives rise to the conviction that love absorbs duty: the law becomes useless in the relationship between human beings and God: 'Love, and do what you like,' said Augustine. It is impossible for freedom arising out of grace and the order of the law to exist side by side in a meaningful way over a long period. Grace is not an addition to the law, its framework; it is its negation, standing outside any rational system; it cocks a snook at justice (cf. the parable of the workers in the vineyard).

Theologies too have given up trying to explain the co-existence: they take refuge in the mystery of divine decisions (predestination). As for the institutional churches, they are of necessity guardians of an order – since every institution is a constraint – but they sail under the banner of the gospel, the reason for their existence. Even if the churches long stood in the way of direct access to the gospel, it nevertheless remains the fact that every believer, from the simplest to the most knowledgable, is convinced that there is no common factor – indeed there is discord – between institutional church order and the irrationality of the gift of God, grace.

In fact, in giving grace or the Spirit God did not stipulate that he would manifest himself uniquely through church institutions or even the sacraments. No church rejects the possibility that he can enter into communication with anyone, that is to say with any believer. But in that case what is the value of institutional criteria? Who is to say that communication with God is true and not proud folly? Who will discern the gift of grace from pretensions to this gift? If the church judges on the basis of institutional criteria, it judges God and the law determines grace. But if each person decides for himself, if the sole criteria is the subjective feeling of divine authenticity, that is to say the declaration of the one who hears the voice of God in himself or herself, what use are the institutional churches? The churches administer grace when they submit to the law, but then they deny it: the churches mediate its freedom or irrationality only by domesticating it, that is to say by destroying it. To want to distribute grace fairly is to deny its essence: it is unfair, unjust.

Coping with this contradiction explains the rise of spiritual movements and modernisms in the churches. These movements are not pathological; they are normal phenomena within churches divided between the institutional order and the freedom of the gospel which they claim to promote. The spiritual movements, constantly forced to abandon their freedom so that the institutional order may live, constantly seek new forms of expression. They are phenomena symptomatic of the 'contradictory' nature of the church: to want to socialize and rationalize in an institution that which is of an 'irrational' order. In short, law and grace cannot be synthesized; so it is not surprising that Christians should constantly emerge for whom the institution limits the freedom of the gospel.

That is Kolakowski's theory. By its very schematism it shows us what we saw earlier when we looked at *Lumen Gentium*: how does one affirm an absolute equality in the church without specifying its institutional forms? How, for instance, does one see that women enjoy equality and the same rights as men in the churches when their sex excludes them by nature from all involvement in its government? Talking of absolute equality or the sovereign freedom of grace can only pose radical problems to the institution.

Kolakowski's theory lays out schematically, in the form of a dilemma, what we have seen in the text from Vatican II: the parallelism between on the one hand the mystery lived out by the people in the Spirit and on the other the hierarchical constitution of the church. The harmony between these two dimensions is postulated by their origin in Christ. As a result, harmony is affirmed in a voluntaristic way: it only gives place to conflict in the order of sin.

Kolakowki's theory has the clarity and the inconveniences of the form of the dilemma: it endorses either the freedom of the gospel, i.e. the mystical option, or the society of the church, the institutional option. It forgets an element which acts as a third function, the sacrament.

It seems to me that this element makes it possible to find a way out of the institutional antinomies often summed up in the contrast between 'people to govern and governors'. The introduction of a common term for both, sacramentality, credits the institution with a function of distancing from the kingdom, a function which is necessary for the truth of our condition and the authenticity of our freedom.

In fact the sacrament has a place in what it is convenient to call the symbolic order.[26] This opens up the way to the idea of a provisional church: on the one hand it postulates that the 'real' (God, the kingdom) cannot enter into our possession in this world; it is a point of escape. So the symbolic order indicates that the church is not yet the kingdom: it looks after the distance necessary for the journey towards it. On the other hand the symbolic order indicates that personal freedom and that of the group are only capable of realization in the form of a 'lack': not possessing the kingdom, not laying hands on God.

So if the sacrament announces and symbolizes that the church is not the kingdom, if it is the place for maintaining its openness to a future, there cannot be any question of thinking of institutionality in the order of fullness, presence: it is the witness to the distance we are from the promised kingdom, and denotes the church as a society in evolution, that is to say as an imperfect or political society. The operative schema of the theology of the Counter-Reformation was that of the 'perfect society': this theology saw the earthly church as the realization of a utopia from which it banished all impurities such as conflicts, evolutions, history.

The constitution *Lumen Gentium* is still fraught with this image of 'fullness': it speaks of 'presence' where it is discussing 'sacred power'. Now it is a matter of 'representation'. Only a perfect society, the realization of ecclesial utopia, the mystical body and its fulfilment would have no need of 'representation': the immediacy of the presence of the Spirit makes every institution unnecessary. This rules out, for our human condition, the impossible dream of immediacy: the kingdom announced by Jesus is not of this world (John 18.36). The hierarchy in the church also originates from the sacrament: in practice it declares the absence of the kingdom; it does not make it present.

The schema of the ideal harmony which is used in Vatican II tends to produce the dilemma analysed by Kolakowski. Either believers aspire to mystical fusion and as a result the gift of the Spirit, by its immediacy, excludes all institutions and all history. Or the institution is an adequate representation of the kingdom: all evolution and all conflict are to be punished by excommunication.

These two options are fatal: either they abolish the provisional character of the church by imagining a heavenly society or they think in terms of the model of the imperfect society, political society. It is the place where the risks of everyday conduct are open to an unsuspected future. We must now consider the work of this future in the historical church.

III

The Church, a Mystical Reality

Since it is historical and institutional, the church is a social and empirical fact, a possible object of scientific investigation like any other empirical fact. It is the context for the exercising of force, conflicts and evolution, all of which bear witness that it does not escape the specific laws of societies. For an objective spectator nothing seems to support the affirmation that it derives from an order different from that of other institutions apart from the ends that it has in view, the ideology of which it is a vehicle and the awareness that it has of itself. It claims to be of a different order by virtue of its objectives, which are to anticipate the kingdom; its ideology, the message of the gospel; and its awareness that it has its origin in the fundamental action of Easter: the resurrection of Jesus and the gift of the Spirit. Its objectives, ideology and awareness call for the description of the institutional and historical society in terms of attributes which are not immediately empirical. In fact since the first Council of Constantinople in 381 the church has confessed itself 'one, holy, catholic (universal) and apostolic' (Denziger 86). Theologians call these descriptions 'marks of the church'. By 'marks' they mean 'distinctive signs or characters'.

These 'marks' were invoked in the polemic of the Counter-Reformation to provide recognition in the midst of all the separate empirical churches of which was the true church, the one which could claim without falsehood to correspond to the intention of Christ. So recently these 'marks' have become significant for apologetic: the church which could pride itself on these four characteristics was indisputably the true church. With the birth and growth of ecumenical dialogue the 'marks' have lost their apologetic aspect: in Catholicism one hardly ever comes acoss theologians who try desperately to prove that the Roman church is the only one to represent these four qualifications validly. So there is a move towards a 'mystical' interpretation of the confession of the Constantinopolitan creed. It is still necesessary to specify what one understands by this fluid term and not end up with a radical separation between the empirical churches and their transcendent qualifications.

To shed light on this difficult question I shall establish the significance of the 'marks', make their status more specific, indicate their ecumenical function and finally define their connection with the empirical churches.

1. The significance of the 'marks' of the church

As a starting point for reflection I suggest the following apparently paradoxical hypothesis: the 'marks' apply in a certain way to the visible churches, but as at a distance and with reticence. We must evaluate the significance of this distance and this reticence.

The aim of this hypothesis is to exclude an inappropriate use of the 'marks' for purposes of demonstration: they presuppose identity between an empirical church and the qualities of the church confessed in the creed. The history of the churches and ecumenical concern tell against an operation which does not take into account the actual plurality of the churches and which obliges one to think that this plurality belongs only in the order of defect and sin. To show that only a particular visible church is truly described as one, holy, universal and apostolic is to exclude any other church from the sphere of the church context and to define its conversion as capitulation.

The hypothesis suggested here will seem more well-founded once I have briefly described each of the 'marks'.

The church is 'one'

The first quality that the confession of faith attributes to the church is that of unity. This 'mark' has its roots in the New Testament. Some texts are very clear on the question; I shall give a brief review of them.

Ephesians 4.1-6 gives us a summary of the convictions scattered through the New Testament. The text of I Cor.1.10-31 warns against dissensions among Christians and exhorts them to be united on the one foundation, Christ. In rather a different context, in I Cor.12, Paul recalls the unity of the Spirit in the diversity of gifts. The church forms a body made up of many members. In Gal.3.27ff. the apostle stresses that all are one in Christ without any distinction of race, social position and sex. The same doctrine underlies the conviction expressed in Rom.12.3-8: the many form one body in Christ. With different images, Luke in Acts 2.42 describes the unity of the church by recalling its practices: perseverance in the apostolic teaching, brotherly communion, breaking of bread, unanimous prayer. John (10.16) stresses both the guarantor of unity, the one shepherd, and his effect, one flock. He grounds this unity (John 10.17-26) on that which prevails between the Father and the Son. In short, the New Testament denotes the unity of the church in terms of the one whom it recognizes as its God – one God the Father, one Lord, one Spirit – and describes this unity in terms of a practice that can be observed: one baptism, one eucharist.

This stress on unity does not dissuade the New Testament authors from speaking of the plurality of churches: they mention the church at Jerusalem, at Corinth, at Antioch. So unity exists at the level of the local church, but on one condiiton: that this church should be in communion with other local churches.

That is the description that can be drawn from the New Testament: it masks serious conflicts, since the historical reality was different. In fact two major decisions mark the history of the church: the schism between East and West and the break at the Reformation. The unity of the church is presented as the New Testament ideal since none of those who confess one Lord is ready to share the same table.

Hence the use of unity as a characteristic made by the creed leads to a paradox: churches claiming the same Lord find themselves separated precisely by virtue of their adherence to him. The specific sanction of this faithfulness is represented by an inability to be in communion. One can understand the temptation to restate the paradox as a simple conviction: any other church than one's own is inauthentic. By contrast, the ecumenical solution is complex: all the churches have elements which postulate unity.

The position of Vatican II is hesitant: there is talk of separated brethren, churches in the plural, and the Catholic church and the church of Christ are no longer identified. In short there is great caution towards anything that could harm ecumenical dialogue, but the Council does not provide elements which allow one to think of the original character of this broken unity.

The church is holy

The second 'mark', that of the holiness of the church, raises similar difficulties to the first. The Vatican II Constitution on the Church (*Lumen Gentium* §39-40) affirms the holiness of the church on a twofold basis: its source is holy since it is God, Christ and the Spirit; the church calls men and women to sanctification; it has the means of bringing about conversion by the gift of the Spirit, the reading of scripture, the celebration of the sacraments and ethical practice.

The Constitution does not say that the members of the visible church are individually and collectively holy; it holds that the visible church represents a symbolic device leading to holiness by virtue of the gift of God.

These specific statements are important; they avoid dishonest interpretations. In fact they allow the rejection on the one hand of sectarian interpretation in which the church is envisaged as a society of the pure, as with the Gnostics, Montanists, Novatians, Cathari, etc., and on the other hand of the idealist interpretation in which the church is collectively declared to be holy but its members are seen as sinners.

The Constitution *Lumen Gentium* regards the church as holy by virtue of its origin, its means and its goal. This declaration does not do away with the question of the ethical or religious value of the historical actions of the churches. Only accord with the demands of the gospel brings sanctification, and no one on earth can be a judge in this matter. Actions are not holy because they are performed by the earthly church. If things are as *Lumen Gentium* says, apologetic polemic about the respective holiness of provisional churches is a waste of time. The degree of holiness of the churches cannot be the subject of an empirical investigation. So there can be no question of establishing a hierarchical order among them.

The church is 'catholic' or universal

The third 'mark' of the true church uses a difficult term. It no longer just denotes the Roman church as the usual vocabulary suggests. It has a wider meaning. In fact its ancient usage is very ambiguous. The term appears only once in the New Testament, in adverbial form, and means 'entirely or totally'. The silence of the New Testament goes well with the many ways in which this 'mark' has been interpreted. Since Christian antiquity the term has had a more precise significance: thus in Ignatius of Antioch (Smyrn.8.2) 'catholic' denotes the whole of the church as a communion of local churches, a meaning which was kept alive in Orthodoxy but which was eliminated in the West from the fourth century on in favour of a more legalistic notion. Thus for the Theodosian Code of 380 the Catholic church represents the state church, the only legitimate one. So catholic denotes legitimate, orthodox belief, protected by the law of the Roman state. This is a legal sense which was to find a dogmatic foundation in the definition put foward by Vincent of Lérins (*Commonitorium* I,2; PL 50, 640) in the fifth century. According to him, 'catholic is that which has been believed everywhere at all times by all people'. In that case 'catholic' denotes the apparently simple criterion of diachronic (historical) and synchronic (geographical) unanimity.

Like the 'mark' of unity, the 'mark' of catholicity, in the sense of communion, orthodoxy or empirical unanimity, poses a difficult problem by reason of the historical divisions which arose between the churches. What church can claim to be 'catholic' in the threefold sense which appeared in history? Does the unanimist interpretation, which turns out in practice to be a majority, have any meaning other than violence? In the last resort the earliest (diachronically) and largest (majority) church defines the truth, so the notion of orthodoxy is formal. As to Catholicity in the sense of communion between the churches, it has not been realized in history. By its political implication, the legal significance could not redeem the failure of the two former senses. So it is against the background of the actual division of the churches that this 'mark', like that of unity, has to be rethought.

The church is 'apostolic'

Apostolicity is the 'mark' which was the subject of the hardest discussions. It seemed to Roman apologists to be the easiest one to use to demonstrate the inauthenticity of the churches which came into being at the Reformation. It was then understood by the defenders of the Roman church in the sense of 'ministerial continuity', the succession of bishops forming an unbroken chain from the time of the apostles. This material approach is inadequate.

To declare the church 'apostolic' is primarily to make this declaration about all the church and not only about a means which it gives itself for realizing its aim, namely the ministry. By that I mean that what was the privilege of the apostles (the New Testament), to be the witnesses of the risen Christ and to teach the word of the gospel with authority – a privilege which cannot be handed down as such – is translated into the task and the mission entrusted by them to the church, that of being itself witness to the gospel. The church is 'apostolic' to the degree that it is founded on the witness of the apostles. It is also on the level of the truth of witness to Christ that apostolicity is demonstrated. However, since this witness takes different forms and includes a ministry (sacrament, pastorate, teaching), there is good reason for describing the episcopal ministry as the heir of the apostles, all the more so where it is in conformity with the task and the mission which were those of the apostles. The polemic between Protestants and Catholics was too orientated on the one ministry (bishops, successors of the apostles). The Reformation questioned the view that material and genealogical continuity ensures apostolic authenticity by virtue of the faults of the church of its time. It believed that authentic apostolicity derived from the Spirit through fidelity to the first witness. This fidelity at different levels of the church is the definition of 'apostolicity'. So it could not be reduced to a material criterion which can be empirically discovered and which allows a completely objective view of the true church.

2. The status of the 'marks' of the church

An empirical, historical, visible and institutional church cannot correspond to the four characteristics that the Niceno-Constantinopolitan creed attributes to the church. It is only by evasions that one can regard one of these qualities as having been realized: the church is not one, although churches have elements of unity without effective communion among themselves; the church is not holy, since its history is marked by its faults; it is not universal, since communion has not been achieved among those who claim to derive from Christ. As to apostolicity, it is a mark of all the churches to the degree that they are faithful to the witness of the apostles, but it would not seem frivolous to want to base the validity of apostolicity simply on material succession: from this perspective the Eastern church would be in a similar position to that of the Roman church.

So if the 'marks' are not empirical or descriptive qualities of the churches, must they be said to be eschatological, i.e. applying to the church of the kingdom or the ideal church?

The eschatological interpretation would appear to be fitting only where description proves impossible. But the eschatological interpretation lacks a qualifying element: a regulative or normative function.

To say that the 'marks' are eschatological and not descriptive is to take account of a break between the earthly church and the kingdom. Now the earthly church, even in its brokenness, must be the sacrament of the kingdom. So it must announce in itself the need for the 'marks' in its present condition. What I mean is that each church is 'church' to the degree that it confesses one God, one Lord, one baptism and one table. The structural elements of which the characteristics are the interpretation are present in the churches, and it is because they are already present in the brokenness, the mediocrity and the particularity that they are internal imperatives of transformation and call for an eschatological realization.

That is why I prefer to say that the 'marks' are not descriptive. No church can boast that it corresponds with them. But they are not simply eschatological – every church lives them out to a limited degree. They are immanent imperatives calling for an overcoming of the break that nothing requires in the logic of structural elements; to overcome the mediocrity that nothing justifies in the proclamation of the gospel; to abandon a closedness which is not based on the message which is proclaimed. In short, they are the structural elements of the church – Word, sacraments, ministries, people – which it is fitting to make immanent structural qualities, realized in a fragmentary way, the imperative of a real practice of collective conversion. In this sense the qualities attributed to the church are the basis of ecumenism.

3. The ecumenical function of the 'marks' of the church

The law of the group is that of exclusion. The church's stake in unity begins from the conviction that every local church is fully the church to the degree that it favours communion with any local church. Thus in terms of the communion of the local churches among themselves one is justified in talking of the universal church. The universal church is not a centralized or federated super-church; it is the result of the communion, that is to say the opening up, of every church. In this way the structural elements of every church, appealing to the imperatives of the creed, find their true régime here.

Now this régime which is described in terms of structural elements (one God, one Lord, one faith, one baptism, one eucharist) cannot be verified in history: the churches which claim to originate from Christ do not share the same view about the demands made by the gospel at the level of the institution and in particular of the ministry. Because of this different estimation, the churches do not think that they can have a common table, i.e. celebrate together the eucharist as a memorial of Christ and in proclamation of the kingdom.

What is scandalous in the situation which has emerged from church history is not the difference in the estimations or the styles of the churches but the fact that these differences get in the way of communion – in short, it is that the churches think that these differences are sufficiently serious and profound on essential matters not to play at being united. So the rejection by the churches of intercommunion is a criterion for the seriousness of the difference.

Now every church which relates to one Lord and performs one baptism *ipso facto* sets out a symbolic device which involves communion, since the symbolic device of every church has a focal point in the eucharist, whether this is understood as sharing in the word, brotherly sharing, or sharing in the body of Christ that makes unity. The present situation of brokenness therefore damages the symbolic device.

This device does not call for a formal, institutional or administrative unity: it essentially calls for a unity of communion. Moreover the demands of the symbolic plan must be represented as conditions: what conditions are required for communion to be possible between the churches, as it was at other times between local churches with different origins and disciplines? The problem of ecumenism, which is vital if the task of the church is to be authentic, arises as these conditions are worked out. The historical transition from war to negotiation, and then to a degree of recognition, implies that no church can now claim to be the place where this communion could be lived out without a transformation of its institutional form and a change in policy. The changes brought about by questioning show this. The Catholic church does not so far want to be officially represented in the World Council of Churches at Geneva, but it has made it known that it is favourable to this enterprise. This situation of entering into negotiation, while not being involved, shows the present ambiguity of the debate: the Roman church is issuing a call for conversion to the other churches that it is not addressing to itself while protesting that the demand affects everyone in the same way. If it took seriously the history of divisions, for which every church is responsible, the Catholic church would consider that for it, too, the characteristics in the creed are imperatives and not descriptions. So it is impossible to demonstrate the ecumenical function of the 'marks' of the church without making an attempt to understand the plurality of the churches theologically.

In fact, as I have indicated, to understand the 'marks' only on the eschatological level, i.e. as denoting the degree of identification between the church and the kingdom, does not correspond to the scriptural demand 'that they all may be one'. As for the other 'marks', they only take specific form to the degree that communion is possible. Now the historical régime is that of a plurality of churches which is experienced as separation. If the kingdom is communion by reason of the gift of the same Spirit which involves each being in a differentiated relationship with the Father, Son and Spirit, it is illogical that the communities charged with this proclamation should make it not in diversity but in opposition, that is to say by appropriating it privately and not sharing it.

The separation derives from an attitude which does not conform to the gift of the Spirit: the impossibility of communion, the sanction of exclusion, presupposes that every church takes to itself the truth of the gospel, thinking that every other church is betraying it. The ecumenical movement arose out of the perception of the need for a movement in the opposite direction: every church is also the place where the gospel is lived out in truth as a questioning of its relationship to the other churches.

If one accepts this hypothesis, separation, the basis of the pluralism of the churches, becomes the means by which each church can justify its claim to be the one true church. This way of understanding the link between pluralism and separation implies that pluralism and a system of exclusion are the same thing. As a result, the return to communion would call for the abolition of pluralism.

Granted, pluralism is the result of historical divisions which resulted in reciprocal excommunications, grave sanctions and sometimes wars. This violent opposition originates in a concern for purification: the divisions were the result. It is through a desire to re-establish the church in the pristine newness of the gospel that the breaks come about. As long as these remain a motive for active separation, they strengthen the claim of each church to define the field of the truth of the gospel. The divisions arise out of a zeal for the truth and are not a sign of either indifference or tolerance. Zeal for the good, heightened through contact with the failures of the church, is the cause of most exclusion.

In this sense the pluralism of the churches, signifying their opposition, in that each believes in all good conscience that it is observing the gospel, is the major failing over the profession of faith in 'one God, one Lord and one Spirit'. The pluralism is not the effect of the Spirit when it is accompanied by this awareness of exclusion. So one can only say that the plurality of opposition has a negative significance: the visible churches are marked by sin and are not the kingdom, since they appropriate the gospel and the Spirit as divisive forces. Such a pluralism is a warning about the authenticity of the practice of each church in terms of the gospel. This type of pluralism sacralizes violence since it finds justification in God.

We must also think of pluralism in positive terms: the ecumenical vision calls for it. It impels each church to take note of its limited truth and its failings. It transforms the significance of the plurality of churches.

The concept of the plurality of the churches is not a univocal concept; it is ambiguous. In the framework of thought which justifies separation it is based either on the conviction that one church deserves this name and all the others are caricatures, or on the feeling that the churches are institutions useful only for the common organization of the group of faithful. They have a practical utility without being related to the kingdom. Hence their plurality makes regional administration necessary.

The ecumenical vision rejects these two interpretations: unity between the churches can be negotiated only if each one in some way deserves the name of the church of Jesus Christ. The Vatican II decree on ecumenism adopts this perspective. As a result, Christians only engage practically in the struggle for unity if they regard this as basic to the proclamation of the kingdom: so they think that the churches are something other than executive institutions for a group with a common interest.

Ecumenical practice is not interested in origins; it confesses before God that each church has a share in the responsibility for pluralism without communion. It is orientated on the future: a unity has to be built the model for which is not at present provided by any church.

This development is not evident to the Catholic church. The Catholic church may judge itself to be the perfect society and therefore identical with the ideal church in its very structure, in which case it thinks that ecumenical practice is a tactical matter. This practice is of a moral, diplomatic and political order aimed at eliminating the false obstacles perceived by non-Catholics. In this view ecumenism would consist in encouraging the return of non-Catholics to the Catholic church. This tactic is an astute operation: it substitutes the violence of diplomacy for the armed violence of the sixteenth and seventeenth centuries. Alternatively, the Catholic church judges itself to be imperfect even in its structure and recognizes that a policy aimed at unity calls for substantial transformations for all the partners in the church. So it admits that it has yet to realize the form of unity, that this unity will be a creation and not a return to things as they were before. That presupposes a dialogue in the truth and a rejection of its own security. Not to define the future in advance is the most difficult demand made by ecumenism to the institutional Catholic group. However, it is nevertheless the condition. Therefore the plurality of the churches has a different sense from that conveyed in separation which is justified by a zeal for goodness and truth. Practice invites Christians to think positively about plurality as an empirical condition for communion.

The churches are plural in the New Testament, but they are in communion. The churches become plural in the course of history through opposition and exclusion: they appropriate the truth of the gospel in a private way. In the ecumenical approach, pluralism ceases to be opposition, since the condition for negotiation is the renunciation of private appropriation. Therefore unity can only be a result; it is not given in a pre-established model. There were moments of unity through communion, but there has not been an eternally valid model of unity. So pluralism is to be thought of positively in the time of the ripening of the kingdom and is not to be judged in negative terms. Let me explain. In a communion of local churches the function of the Bishop of Rome could be rethought. The definition of the status and role of the Pope could take account of the unrealized institutional unity of the empirical churches. It would include the fact that neither the New Testament nor church history provide models.

Organizational unity, which is a dominant feature of Latin Christianity, has shown its incapacity to keep local churches in communion: it did away with too many specific legitimate rights. The present plurality of the churches bears witness to the impasse to which organizational unity leads. Unless there were a suggestion for a form of unity for the churches through multiple cultural involvement, the present situation would remain preferable to an organizational unity which would be almost inevitably fixed or repressive. It is beneficial because it no longer engenders opposition but promotes competition based on a respect for differences and working to inaugurate a communion which is no longer formal but real. Paradoxically, the ecumenical approach is now the basis for the future of a differentiated unity. From this perspective ecumenism is orientated on a future that no church would be capable of producing of itself, i.e. independently of others.

The numerous disputes which have arisen in the Catholic church since Vatican II confirm the idea of an internal agitation which is in accord with the urgency of the ecumenical demand. This challenge has attacked the authoritarian institutional practice of the Catholic church. It has reached all the areas where the church had proved to be authoritarian: the expression of faith, morality, the form of worship, disciplinary rules and the organization of church government. It was provoked by the contradiction inherent in this practice: the expression of a universal concern for communion coming up against a centralized form of government. The ideology of collegiality, while favouring a certain form of anarchy, has reinforced the symbolic power of the Pope.

The internal dispute repeats the ecumenical questioning: the transcendental characteristics of the churches give place to the justification of dominant practices and favour exclusion. Whatever may otherwise be the justification for its form, the dispute has shown how difficult it was for the Catholic church to recognize the different relationships to the gospel as being positive and to accept that democracy should be required as its life-style and by its government. These difficulties lead to a more specific definition of the link between the transcendental characteristics of the church, which is their work in its present.

4. The link between the 'marks' of the church and the empirical churches

The ecumenical approach has revived the original significance of the 'marks' of the church. It is an invitation to give a more precise definition of their link with the empirical churches and to try to describe their work. The title of this chapter, 'The Church, a Mystical Reality', suggests that this link is produced by an act of God which goes beyond any control by reason. It seems to me that this would be a failure to understand the meaning of the adjective 'mystical': certainly it denotes the 'spiritual' source of the church and is not opposed to the empirical as one sphere to another: it operates in and by the empirical. It is because the churches have these transcendental characteristics that it is necessary to try to describe the link between the characteristics and the churches and the way that they work in them. If the 'spiritual' cannot be reduced to the rational, it is not opposed to the effort to explain in rational and therefore communicable terms what is evoked 'poetically' by recourse to the experience of a life which cannot be identified with either the manipulable or the ideological. There is a great temptation to mark out a frontier between the empirical and the spiritual, the visible churches and the invisible church: the thought of the believer is called on to pass this test. The following hypothesis will form the starting point for our reflection: by their very witness, the visible empirical churches do not stop at themselves but denote what the New Testament calls the 'kingdom'. The transcendental qualities or 'marks' are a specific way of signifying the church in relation to that towards which they point. Ideas borrowed from secular knowledge or drawn from the New Testament serve, if not to explain, at least to denote the relationship which is established between the ultimate, the kingdom, and the present existence of the church: it may be said that it is a matter of the church as 'ideal', 'utopian' or as an eschatological reality. These designations leave untouched the problem of any link. Now that we have made the vocabulary a bit more specific, this is a question that we must go on to tackle.

First we must make the vocabulary more specific. The words which concern us are 'kingdom', 'ideal', 'utopia' and 'eschaton'.

I shall not go into the discussion about two related words, reign and kingdom. Of a variety of well-documented words it is clear that the term reign is preferable. 'Kingdom' describes a domain, 'reign' denotes an activity. In the preaching of Jesus, the main theme of which is summed up in Mark 1.15, 'The time is fulfilled and the reign of God is at hand', 'reign' denotes the present activity of God, like the act of his forgiveness: there cannot be any question of identifying this reign with visible churches; they doubtless have a relationship with it but they are not identical with it. So the kingdom cannot be reduced to an internalization or ethical rectitude: it gives place to the advent of the kingdom. The question of the link between the churches and the reign of God or the churches and the kingdom (the ultimate kingdom) only arises for the advocates of an *eschaton* which has already been realized[1] – the divine forgiveness and the gift of the Spirit are always in the present – or for the advocates of an *eschaton* to come. In either case the churches are witnesses to that which is coming or will come. The action of God would therefore only be another form of the word.

The terms 'ideal' and 'utopia' are more ambitious: they claim to discern the link by fixing the way in which it works. As for the term *eschaton*, its main aim is to describe a gap between the empirical and that which it announces. The following discussion will be formulated around these three terms.

To think of the qualities attributed to the empirical churches as belonging to an ideal order is to give them a critical and regulatory function; it is not to see them as a context for realization, whether present or to come. Beyond question these 'marks' play this role: in that case the notion of the 'ideal' indicates the difference between what is envisaged and the empirical reality of the churches. The 'marks' keep them in their humble condition while heightening their desire for transformation. The ideal is the unity of the churches, their holiness, the truth of their apostolic witness, and their universality. This ideal is unattainable because it is a pure form, and yet it works in the churches for their conversion. However, the notion of the ideal is not enough to indicate the link between the empirical churches and their transcendent qualities. An ideal is a projection, its status is critical and regulative: it does not denote a content, a position, a reality; it indicates the inherent lack in the empirical and it conveys the disquiet to be found there. In this sense it risks devaluing the ambiguous density of experience for the benefit of a formula which is thought to be 'spiritual'. The ideal is also the form taken by the law to the degree that it represents the internal logic of a social group or an institutional system. It makes it 'relative' and therefore flexible, capable of transformation, dynamic. The ideal 'marks' of the church relativize and dynamize the empirical churches: they are removed from what the churches proclaim themselves to be. It nevertheless remains the case that an 'ideal' is abstract, even if it forms the dynamic for a social group. Now the 'marks' envisage a specific reality: they have the status of evangelical witness to the degree that they are realized in the present. And they are realized in the present to the degree that their specific force does not come only from the empirical church but from an energy which transcends them: the kingdom or the action of God which is always contemporary. The ideal is projection, the kingdom is gift. The kingdom marks out the limit of the explanatory function of this notion in its attempt to provide a link between 'marks' and empirical churches. Moreover, if it is a gift, it is not an empty one, a meaningless energy. As a critical and normative ideal the 'marks' do not specify a content which could serve as a model. Some theologians have thought that a more political concept would allow a better link between the 'marks' and the empirical churches; what they have in mind is the concept of utopia.

5. The eschatological dimension of the 'marks' of the church

The concept of utopia is striking because of its paradoxical character. H. Desroches, paraphrasing Thomas More, has suggested the following description:[2]

Utopia signifies 'nowhere', a place which is not in any place, an absent presence, an unreal reality, a nostalgic elsewhere, an otherness without identification. This name is associated with a series of paradoxes: Amaurote, the capital of the island, is a phantom city; its river, Anyder, a river without water; its chief, Adamus, a prince without a people; its inhabitants, the Alaopolitans, inhabitants without a city, and their neighbours, the Achorians, inhabitants without a country. This philological prestidigitation has the avowed aim of indicating the plausibility of a world in reverse and the latent aim of denouncing the legitimacy of a world supposedly the right way round.

The term utopia was coined by Thomas More in the sixteenth century. However, the birthplace of utopia was Greece (see Plato's *Republic* and *Laws*).

With Christianity, the utopian imagination disappeared for almost fifteen centuries; it was supplanted by messianic agitation. However, it marked certain forms of messianism, like millenarianism: there the kingdom of God is a kingdom of plenty. Moreover utopias have been put into practice: the Feast of Fools in the Middle Ages, the world turned upside down, or the birth of societies outside society (eremitism and monasticism). Again, in the twelfth century Joachim of Fiore dreamed of an age of the Spirit: a perfect generalized monasticism which would absorb church and society.

With the fifteenth and sixteenth centuries, Europe was opened up to other continents. People saw the birth of another cycle of utopias, with Thomas More's *Utopia*, which remained the model, or with Erasmus' *In Praise of Folly* of 1511. Following Thomas More's model, there was a considerable boom in utopias in the nineteenth century. Socialisms of every kind paid homage to this literary genre and this dream which they judged to be subversive. In fact utopia presents itself as the imaginary projection of another society, a reversal of the everyday world. Some examples given in the guise of illustrations bear witness to this logic. Community was substituted for the atomized family. This included sexual sharing, or was an inducement to generalized monasticism. Sexuality in effect lost its mysterious aura; it was organized, deprived of drama.

The same process applied to property. When property is owned privately the result is a redistribution of riches which is so unfair that it provokes violence. In utopia there is nothing of the sort: the ownership of property is common; the economy does not undergo any growth, but simply produces the support necessary for life. The government also tends to disappear: there it represents a simple control of the activities necessary for the support of the city. If power exists it is assigned to a virtuous class. In general this is a self-governing society. The absence of government is related to the perfection of the society. If deviations appear they are neutralized. In short, the organization of the utopian city and its strict rules are aimed at preserving its members from being soiled by the outside world and from internal deviations. Not being faced with any other challenge, the utopian city has no history, since, being a perfect city, it has satisfied all desires.

At least with Thomas More this fiction of another society, radically different from that of its day, conceals some evident contradictions which it is worth pointing out. Thus utopia is the exemplary universal city, but it is based on separation: it is an island separated from the rest of the world. Utopia is also a society without conflict, but it is an armed society, using mercenaries and stratagems to ensure its tranquillity. Utopia is a free city, but so that it can attend to spiritual leisures, it employs slaves. Utopia is a happy society, but it imposes ridiculous constraints. Utopia is a definitive society: it ensures the perpetuity of its institutions but it is in a world in which history exists since it maintains relations with other forms of society.

These contradictions reveal the literary genre: utopia is not a political project to be realized. In fact the reversal of the everyday and the contradictions of the régime are aimed at criticizing the present by means of an imaginary fiction which presents another society outside history, rather than commending a political project for history. It is *qua* fiction that utopia is subversive. It stresses the contingent character of the everyday.

This critical concept did not find a place in theology as easily as one might imagine: utopia is not the New Testament eschaton. Perhaps it is because of a defensive instinct that theology has so far made little use of it. Recent theological dictionaries do not mention it. Vatican II does not make use of it. Its recent use in theology does not do away with the inherent ambiguity of the concept in current language. From being a technical term denoting an 'imaginary country or ideal government reigning over a happy people' which *Petit Robert*, the standard dictionary in French, deems to be an antiquated sense, the term has tended to take on a banal sense: 'Ideal, political and social view which takes no account of reality... A conception or project which would appear impossible to realize.' To this definition *Petit Robert* adds a series of synonyms: 'Chimaera, illusion, mirage, dream, daydream'. The current sense is well defined by a phrase of Victor Hugo: 'A daydream of a visionary inventor, a utopia'.

Introducing so ambiguous a concept into theology at the point when many people judge the effectiveness of the gospel to be the basic question might seem to be provocative. In fact the introduction of this concept marks a change of reference point: the eschaton or the future has so far played an academic or ethical role in theology.

It has been academic in that people did their duty by the creed in a treatise on the so-called last things, which did not affect the theological task as a whole. It has been ethical in that since a society without sanctions had difficulty in subsisting, so that the number of regulations was high and the occasions for transgressing them were many, the result was an inflation in the penalties or rewards in the beyond aimed at securing order in the present world. Under these two rubrics, the future does not operate in a dynamic way by subverting the present; on the contrary, by the use of sanctions or merits it reinforces the present order. Now under the influence of ideologies bound up with technological progress or under the pressure of socialist messianisms, the future has become a dominant category in modern existence. So it proves necessary to reinterpret the Christian message and its witness, the church, under this category. This new horizon of culture does not, however, explain the vogue for the concept of utopia: it has been preferred to that of *eschaton*.

One kind of theology has been attracted to this concept to describe the relationship of the churches to their aim, the kingdom of God, in terms of determinations inherent in its structure. Utopia expresses a revolt against the inhumanity of social conditions in a particular period, but it suspends their effect by reflection: the situation is analysed, the causes producing it are investigated, and means of eliminating it are established. It relates to an imaginary construction around a principle which contradicts this state, the generating principle of hardship: private property in Thomas More, for example. Finally, ideas on how to act are deduced from an analysis of the world as it is and the difference from the world as it should be. If this difference is infinite (absolute contradiction) one really does have a utopia. In this sense utopia is a reasonable idea with no means of realization. It is of an imaginary order.

So for its elaboration utopia requires the convergence of the following factors: a movement of revolt without a sufficient collective base (messianism); the perception of the present folly of all action; a judgment made on contemporary society with reference to an ideal state constructed on the basis of causes leading to the present problems. Thus utopia denotes the present and painful absence of the perfect society. It judges that no anticipation of it is conceivable except in the imagination.

Transferred to theology, the concept of utopia is that by which one can come to think of the eschaton – or the kingdom of God. So by this term one would indicate that the eschaton judges our present on the basis of the revolt against its inhumanity growing within it; that the eschaton could not have any anticipation in this present; that it has no means of action and no promises to establish the kingdom there as a perfect society; that it acts only as an imaginary subversion of the present. These two consequences of the transposition of the eschaton into utopia require historical verification: this could only be given by the way in which the empirical churches have lived out their link with the kingdom.

6. The work of the Ultimate in the present

The question of the link between the churches and the kingdom is historically a complex one because there is no unifying tradition but only provisional attempts at articulation.

The complexity is connected with the fact that the churches have never established any consensus on their link with the kingdom, and this has been the case since late antiquity. This hesitation is connected with the specific character of the underlying questions, which are political, social and even scientific, like the relationship between the kingdom and the future of the universe. The factors involved in any judgment are too different for believers and theologians to be unanimous over them. A historical example may indicate this complexity: at the time when a large part of the church was rejoicing over the conversion of Constantine (312) and saw this as the beginning of the messianic era, some Christians thought that they should break with the world; they emigrated into the desert, stressing by this retreat the vanity of political and religious enthusiasm.

In the modern period complexity produces indecision: where is the supposed link between the churches and the kingdom to be located in the movement of events? Laborious exegesis of 'the signs of the times' highlights the perplexity among believers: they hesitate to define the actions which would hasten the advent of the hoped-for future. It is also all the more necessary to verify the ambiguity of the supposed link by historical investigation. For reasons of brevity I have chosen three elements whch seem to me to be exemplary in the history of the churches in connection with this link: enthusiasm, pessimism and negotiated autonomy. These elements are both historical and structural. They work through an exchange of domination.

Enthusiasm

I use this image to denote the interpretation according to which the link between the churches and the kingdom is presented as a utopia realized in our history: Christ will reign on earth in a rediscovered paradise. The future is thus marked with the seal of a specific reconciliation and a shared abundance, eliminating all anguish and violence. The church is identified with the kingdom in an imminent and earthly future.

The Christian preaching that Jesus the prophet of Nazareth was alive sparked off ambiguous feelings about this world. On the one hand it provoked impatient waiting for his return. One can see signs of it in the letters to the Thessalonians. It led to a devaluation of history, of the here and now, and engendered the calumny that this world was destined to perish. On the other hand it stirred up the no less impatient desire for his beneficial return to earth to transform it in accordance with the social model of the prophecies of Israel, to eliminate relationships which led to social exploitation and to provide an abundance of goods for the righteous.

In this space marked out by the return of Jesus, who would transform our history, what is called millenarianism took root (Rev.

20.1-6). The doctrine is concerned with the link between the church and the kingdom.[3] The sources of this belief and this hope are ancient. Earlier than Christianity, their origin lies in Jewish messianism, the announcement of the reign of a Davidic king who establishes justice and abundance on earth.

Ancient oracles (like Isa.9.1; 11.1; 54.2; Ezek.40-47: Dan.7; 12) provided the basis of this earthly messianism, and later apocalyptic visions, buttressing the ancient prophecies, confirmed it (cf. Jubilees 22; 27; Enoch 61; 62; IV Esdras 7.28). They announced the imminence of a reign which was to last four hundred years.

Rabbis took up these beliefs, harmonizing them with other texts. Thus the four hundred years became a thousand years by reason of the interpretation according to which the six days of creation represented the six thousand years of distressing history and the seventh day the thousand years of happy rest.

This last interpretation found its way into the New Testament (Rev.19-22). It had such a great success that the Christian opponents of millenarianism were led to deny that Revelation was written by John or had a place in the canon in order to support their polemic.

The Jewish hope of an earthly messianism had not been deprived of its prerogatives by the Christian event of the cross and resurrection. On the contrary, this victory of Jesus over the deadly laws of the 'old world' challenged the force of the old belief. It enjoyed a revival as much among those who claimed allegiance to the mainstream church as among those who rejected the major options. Among the latter Cerinthus, who made Jesus an ordinary man, shared the millenarian opinion, describing the world to come with an excessive wealth of detail (Eusebius, *Church History* III, 28, 2; VII, 25,2). The same current of thought gained ground in the great church; evidence of this is to be found in the Letter of Barnabas (XV, 4,9); Justin (*Dialogue*, LXXX), Tertullian (*Against Marcion* IV, XXXIX), Lactantius, third century (*Divine Institutions*, VII 22, 24), and above all Irenaeus of Lyons (*Against the Heresies*, LIV, 5).

Irenaeus attacked heretics who claimed that salvation was to be achieved through flight from the world and knowledge of the secrets of the process of its creation. This knowledge of the origins of the world conveyed by a descending series of intermediaries made it possible, these heretics claimed, to escape our wretched condition and specifically that of bodily existence by going back up the chain in a progressive initiation. For Irenaeus the world is the creation of the one God and is not to be slandered. God, in Christ, will perfect it through transfiguration, specifically of those who have not calumniated it. For God, rejecting nothing that he has made, seeks to restore to a superior state that which has lost the way more by ignorance than by ill will. Irenaeus calls the way in which God brings human beings to intimacy with him 'the economy of God' (I, 10,3; II, 4,1). Since God is the Blessed One, it is to share his blessedness with humanity that he acts through his prophecies and his Christ. However, human beings, accustomed as they are to wretchedness, cannot immediately bear the divine bliss. To become familiar with God they must also become familiar with bliss. It is also for this reason that, by pedagogy, God has provided for a twofold initiation into bliss and a twofold fulfilment for humanity.

The human being is not just a spirit or a soul: what he or she suffers in the body cannot be restored by spiritual bliss; there is also need for bodily joy. Belonging to the world, human beings are subjected to the misfortunes of all kinds of exploitation and deprived of the joys which they might claim. It is also right that God should make them so that they may enjoy this world created for their bliss.

Irenaeus borrows the form of this fulfilment from Revelation (19-22): Christ will reign on earth in terrestrial abundance and joy, far from all threats, leading human beings to come to learn the bliss that they will ultimately find in the contemplation of the divine countenance.

It should be noted that this millenarian hope in Irenaeus is based solely on belief in the divine goodness; it is not bound up with an investigation of our history. It would be to misunderstand the thought of Irenaeus to see in millenarianism a controversial political doctrine.

The political idea emerged later, at the time of the triumph of Constantine. Eusebius of Caesarea was one of its best protagonists. He signed the death warrant of millenarian enthusiasm. For Eusebius, in writing a history of the church from the beginnings to the victory of Constantine in 312, thought that he had to see in it the fulfilment of the divine plan of history.

So Eusebius does not share the millenarianism of Irenaeus. He thinks that Irenaeus is a dreamer. It is unthinkable that Christ should exercise on earth a power analogous to political power so as to procure abundance without work. For Eusebius, the kingdom here below presupposes intermediaries: it is fulfilled in human terms.

Eusebius the historian refers to real events and not to dreams arising out of a desire for rest and abundance. But he sees in these events indications of the providential action of God on the basis of a twofold conviction. On the one hand he shares the pagan idea that the king is a god for the state, as God is God for the universe. The king is the practical incarnation of wisdom and law for men since he is the god for this world. Like his predecessor Philo, Eusebius banishes any temptation towards idolatry: it is not the person of the king which is invested with divine honour but his function.

The role of the king and emperor is thus basically sacred, and in this sense royal politics is a reflection of the divine will.

But on one condition: that the king be 'wise', i.e. that he should be the effective practitioner of the divine law.

With the accession of Constantine to the empire, on the one hand the old Hellenistic ideal of the king as the image of God was achieved since the emperor did not desire other than to apply the law of Christ. After several centuries of opposition between Christianity and empire, this victory was inevitably seen as the indication of the last times, the irruption of the long-awaited kingdom.

On the other hand, Eusebius remains stamped by Jewish prophetic messianism: he waits for the fulfilment of the prophecies for this world – but not as Irenaeus expected it, by a constant miracle – he waits for it through the accession to power of a leader who will make the empire a haven of peace and justice. The Roman empire is in fact the last empire according to Daniel. Converted, it will allow Christianity to produce its earthly fruits.

Here one can see all the difference between the millenarianism of an Irenaeus, who expects nothing of the empire and politics and makes Christ exercise a direct political reign after the first resurrection, and the thought of Eusebius, who sees in the empire and the politics of his converted emperor the realization of the messianic promises, before the tribulations which will usher in the ultimate advent of the kingdom beyond this world.

Millenarianism virtually disappeared in the fourth century after the victory of Constantine, when the empire became Christian. Doubtless Constantine's conversion was seen as the realization of what had been expected, formerly expressed in images and symbols.

But what many people expected as an immediate reign of Christ was in fact a political reign, with all the consequences which stemmed from the fact that Christianity had in this way become a doctrine which inspired and sacralized politics.

Thus of the utopian dream of Irenaeus and the realism of Eusebius, it was the latter which came out on top, politics having appropriated the dream for its own benefit without finally producing the expected fruits. The empire was not the place of justice and peace. The Christians in power embarked on their career with an intolerance towards pagan cults against which some bishops stood out. Even after the empire had disappeared, the latent desire of Eusebius for harmony between politics and church anticipating the ultimate kingdom exercised its influence down to our days. The failure of the Christian empire has taught us that the baptism of princes and the support that they bring the church is not enough to eliminate the injustice of the world and to banish exploitation. The dream of Irenaeus gained new vigour in movements of popular revolt inspired by the Bible, the peasant revolts, the brothers of the free spirit, the Franciscan dream of a new world in America, the revolt of Thomas Müntzer, and so on. The dream remained a hidden ferment, the protest of the Christian conscience at the confiscation of the authority of Christ by the princes. Neither millenarianism nor political Christianity define the work of the Ultimate in the church's present.

Pessimism

The triumph of the Christian empire and the promulgation of laws which were not pagan did not resolve social problems, political problems or religious dissension. Through clumsiness and intolerance their effect was to lead numerous pagans to accuse Christians of having brought about the collapse of the empire: the fall of Rome sparked off this process of accusation. Augustine's work *The City of God* arose out of his personal anguish and the disarray which affected Christians confronted with the sombre political future.[4]

The City of God is a long meditation on the relationship between the two cities, that which comes from the righteous Abel and that which comes from Satanic pride. Augustine presents a dramatic vision of the struggle between good and evil, a struggle which will only come to an end with the arrival of new heavens and a new earth by the omnipotent action of God. There is no utopian place in this world where only good reigns. The just have no dwelling place here, but are on pilgrimage.

Thus there disappeared the idea of a place anticipating the kingdom here and now: we have a struggle between protagonists determined by subjective factors, love and egoism. For Augustine, the kingdom germinates in this world, but he rejects all experimental, social or political knowledge of it. It is not the earthly church since the two cities dispute it and cross it. The kingdom is ethical and theological. Augustine's view of the separation of the two cities and his refusal to assign them tangible spheres before the last judgment had a considerable spiritual and theological future in all the churches. Paradoxically this opinion, because of its dramatic pessimism about the world, contributed towards reinforcing the ideas of Eusebius, which then took the form of political Augustinianism. If our world is doomed to tragedy and if evil is active everywhere, the laws, buttressed by the powers of the church and the state, must be sufficiently good to hold back the proliferation of evil. Certainly neither church nor state is the kingdom: their duty is to allow it to grow both in individuals and in institutions. There is a slide towards the notion of Christendom: it makes the visible church the antici-patory guarantee of the kingdom where it imposes its law on society. Thus Christendom is born as much from the pessimism of Augustine as from the views of Eusebius. Only the dismantling of Christendom allowed the conception of other forms of relationship between the world, the church and the kingdom.

Negotiated autonomy

Christendom collapsed and produced the fruits of division. The states seized their autonomy and detached themselves from the tutelage and the norms of the church; they gave themselves purely secular aims under the influence of secular ideologies. Entry into the kingdom or its coming seemed to have no link with political and social movements. The kingdom belongs to the private sphere or the moral domain: the church, which announces it, becomes marginalized in society. However, pressure from a secular messianism, Marxism, brought back the problem of the overall collective relationship between the church and history.

The Reformation and then the division of the churches had considerable repercussions on relations between the church and the world. From now on no church any longer had illusions about its provisional status: the churches knew from experience that they were not the kingdom of God. The kingdom has not come in history in them or through them; nor has it come in the world.

The social sanction of divisions, the roots of which preceded actual divisions, was the recession. From the seventeenth century, Christian ideals were attacked. This recession gradually showed itself in terms of a loss of real, ideological and political power. The ideas of Eusebius and Augustine could still be the objects of dreams or theories, but they ceased to be effective.

The Catholic church had difficulty in adapting to the new situation: it took three centuries for it to accept its modest place. But from the time when it renounced political power it decided to play a spiritual role and addressed even the non-Christian world on the moral and social plane (cf. the social encyclicals of popes Leo XIII, Pius XI, John XXIII, Paul VI and the constitution *Gaudium et Spes* of Vatican II). Thus the Catholic church, renouncing a display of political power, claimed a moral leadership not only for Christians but for humanity.

It is within this situation that the virtually messianic attempts at liberation theologies and the work of Christians for socialism take place. It is thought that Christianity can translate itself into a secular form by reason of its utopian dynamism.

This effacement of the church, this concern to incarnate in the secular the utopia of the reign of freedom and brotherhood ceaselessly revives a problem which has to be faced by both the official leadership and the basic communities: how can one have some influence on the world in such a way that utopia ceases to be a dream? The church is historically torn between two temptations: that of becoming a political force and that of escaping into the spiritual realm. Is the idea of a prophetic vocation which removes this twofold temptation acceptable and realistic? The political, cultural, economic and technological revolutions in which we are involved explain the current uncertainty. There is no theological force which can get us over a situation which determines us. If theology is uncertain, that is doubtless because it belongs to the very future of being.

This brief historical enquiry undertaken to investigate the basis of ideas formed to elucidate the relationship between the empirical churches and the kingdom, between their mystical aspect and their tangible reality, indicates the unsatisfactory character of two of them, the ideal and utopia.

On the one hand there have been dreams of utopia imposed on the world (millenarianism) or built up within it (Christendom). These forms of utopia have proved to be deceptive: the former because it does not take into account real history as a place of transformation but relates to a purely supernatural history, the latter because while taking account of real history and clashing with it, it sought to force it by violence to be the social anticipation of the kingdom. On the other hand, the autonomy arising out of modernity which followed this twofold disappointment favoured the emergence of a normative utopia, but of a purely secular kind and one which no longer corresponds to the gospel.

This work of the future in the churches' present must therefore be thought of in other terms, precisely because of that to which the churches relate, the gospel. In fact the gospel proclaimed by the churches does not propose any social planning: that is determined by actual facts. It makes a demand: there is no way to God where justice fails to be done to human beings, to the outcast. This has given rise to the theme of the poor as the critical point of society. But the gospel does not determine the forms of law; it articulates the promise of the Spirit.

These facts allow us to envisage the future in the present situation of the earthly churches in an original way. First, in a negative fashion: the future in the present situation of the earthly churches does not imply that they have control of a utopia, a form of successful planning of social relationships which produces happiness. In this sense they know nothing of planning for the future, whether this concerns history or after history (the Ultimate). All projection of the kingdom outside history is a projection of desires, an infinitization: at that point it forgets the gift of God as otherness and therefore requires purification.

They also allow us to envisage the future in a positive way: the future in the church's present is buttressed on the one hand by sacramentality and the gift of the Spirit and on the other hand by their practice.

To take sacramentality first: the churches, by their very structure, represent a symbolic device suggesting another life; this is denoted by the image of the new birth. Baptism evokes birth in the Spirit. This latter opens up another dimension, that immanent to the call of the gospel. 'Sacramentality' does not relate immediately to a future but evokes the difference in the present. It is here and now that the Spirit brings about new birth, that is to say allows access to another life (Rom.6.8). Hence the term 'utopia' is no longer suitable: the action of the Spirit is not imaginary; it is action bringing about conversion, and conversion has within it the seeds of the kingdom.

In practice the churches are structured by a symbolic device signifying by the gift of the Spirit access to another life (new birth). A symbolic device is neither imaginary nor formal: it is a call for action. The churches in their provisional conditions are also at the same time the place of risky experimentation and questioning depending on this symbolic device.

They are the place of risky experimentation: they are subject to the imperative that the social relationships existing between them should be in accord with the symbolic device that they bear. So people talk of the church as communion. This is not a matter of idealism but of real demands: first those of the outcast, the poor, of equality before God; those signified by the marks of the church: oneness, holiness, universality. If the symbolic device included in the sacrament is confined to the cultic sphere it is betrayed: it implies a social surface which is variable and not planned, but real. In this sense the present demand of communities which are places of recognition and experimentation correspond well to the symbolic device.

The churches are a place of questioning: the difference between the churches and the state, the secular world, is the condition of their truth as churches which cannot be identified with the kingdom. But this difference also signifies that the world is not the kingdom. Nor can it be, in that it does not include vital space for the nonentity, the poor. Hence the symbolic device which structures the churches hurts this world, and practical Christianity does not consist in putting in train utopian planning but in bringing to light effectively the fact that societies, whether or not they are planned, exist at the expense of those whom they reject. The motive power for the transformation of all society is the refusal to accept as fatal the production of exclusion. So the kingdom hurts all social sufficiency, but does so in order to achieve a transformation into precise action in every situation.

The churches only hurt civil society in this way if they have the same effect on their own empirical reality. The word of the gospel does not provide them with the theoretical and practical means of organizing a society. It is precisely in this sense that neither they nor the kingdom that they proclaim are utopian. No one could deduce from the Ultimate and the gospel a society in which the equation of justice and happiness was achieved. That is why the term utopia does not seem to me to illuminate the relationship between the empirical churches and the kingdom, through its reversal of conditions which are, however, made specific in relation to our societies. The term 'mystical', when linked with 'prophetic', has the advantage of denoting the internal difference in the reality of the churches, their critical possibilities, by reason of the distance that they do not cease to proclaim from what they preach and try to put into practice by their conversion, namely the kingdom of God.

The churches are provisional societies; they live out the kingdom in accordance with a symbolic device which requires them to undergo a collective conversion aimed at instituting social relationships which do not lead to exclusions, and questioning all society which produces outcasts either by planning or by indifference.

I would add that to derive from the symbolic device of the churches the need for the integration of the outcast within social relationships does not imply any justification of failure or waste in history. The relationship of the earthly churches to the kingdom does not make the whole of history intelligible. The study of their provisional character will bear witness to the authenticity of their mystical reality as signified by the marks of the church in the creed: one, holy, catholic and apostolic.

IV

The Provisional, the Symbolic and the Kingdom

The course we have followed prompts us to make a qualified judgment on the empirical churches: sometimes in greatness and often in indecision they bear witness to the advent of the kingdom, but they are not that kingdom. The hypothesis which emerges from the recognition of the historical, institutional and mystical character of the churches can be summed up in this way: the more they accept the provisional character of their forms, their structures and their strategies, the closer they come to the kingdom and the better they bear witness to it. In this last chapter I must also elucidate the links which are being forged in the empirical churches between the provisional character of their forms, the symbolic value of their structures and the ultimate aim of their witness: the coming of the kingdom. The course should be clear: in the first section I shall dwell on what I mean by provisional; in the second on its link with what I call the symbolic; and in the third I shall bring all this together around witness to the Ultimate, the coming of the kingdom. Elements already studied in earlier chapters will here be integrated into the wider context of the interpretation of ecclesiology.

1. The provisional in the churches

Our study of the history of the churches in the first chapter should have familiarized us with a dimension which hardly goes with spontaneous reaction to the religious sphere in terms of the place of the manifestation of the transcendent. The link between the Absolute and objects, social forms, ritual actions and functions of responsibility automatically confers on them a stability and intangibility which even in fragile time have the solidity of the eternal. To acknowledge that the elements which give tangible form to the churches are themselves provisional might seem to be a misunderstanding of the desire inherent in the demand for the sacred and the immutability of the Absolute. Without the acceptance of the provisional character of the forms of the church, any affirmation of their historicity is empty. A recognition of the provisional element, that is to say of the capacity for change and innovation in the form of the churches, is the test of the acceptance of 'having to die' so that the kingdom can be born.

However, an objection arises: the provisional in the churches does not seem as though it should affect the totality of its forms. Certain things are said to be so much part of the permanent structure of the institution that to describe them as provisional would amount to depriving them of all symbolic value in the context of the Ultimate. To express that with more clarity and in a more classical language, to describe as provisional, at least in the Catholic church, the sacramental symbolism over which the authorities claim to have no control, would amount to eliminating the effective aim of sacramentality in favour of a constant effort at creation in order to express, at least in a particular situation, the collective relationship with the risen Christ and the advent of the kingdom. The variation in the forms and their provisional character would stop when it was a matter of the symbolism of the kingdom. That would define forms, whether ritual or even hierarchical, which in essence escape the provisional. Hence the link that is sought would not be based on a balance of variables but on stable points of reference which it would be the task of the churches to safeguard in the midst of the movement of history. Certainly there would be a provisional element, but it would represent the froth on the permanent repetition of an identical symbolism in the instability of time. In that case the forms of the church would not be provisional, except in a hyperbolic form of expression.

These objections call for further explanation of the provisional but do not require us to abandon this category. In fact the claim that the churches are provisional does not arise so much out of a purely sociological analysis of the variations between them as out of a quest for their mystical or eschatological goal. An example should make this statement clearer.

The Provisional, the Symbolic and the Kingdom

In Christian faith the conviction of the resurrection does not eliminate the destruction brought about by death. Death is not a fact external to human nature, affecting only part of oneself. It marks its end since it removes the possibility of intercommunication. Christian faith which affirms the radical character of death, since no one can regain his or her life, simply says that by the action of God the risen one is in a certain continuity with his historical life. Without this continuity it would have to be argued that before God the just and the unjust are alike. Historical life is provisional, but it is not unrelated to what would classically be called the eternal. *Mutatis mutandis* the same would be true of the churches. As historical realities they are marked by death; they nevertheless sustain a link with the kingdom. It is the specific character of this link which must be clarified in terms of the provisional character of the historical churches.

The provisional denotes the fact that the churches are historical and therefore mortal; it is not a pejorative judgment, suggesting a lack of value. The performance of a Beethoven sonata, the showing of a film, are provisional. To recognize this does not detract from the beauty of the sonata or the quality of the film. The provisional denotes the condition of innovation, of continual creation, of presence in changing situations: it is opposed to a stubborn concern to stop the moment, the mobility of forms or the mortality of relationships. The provisional also affects all the forms which are historical in the churches: organization, social forms, symbolic forms, doctrinal expressions. In affecting them, it does not shut them up in the moment but opens them up towards their goal, the coming of the kingdom.

The provisional affects the organization of the church: this feature can easily be accepted if the organization only amounts to incidental arrangements made by the institution: it is less so once there is a suspicion that it involves institutional forms.

The organization of a church is the product of a memory and a contemporary challenge. The Catholic church has a very complex organization. In a link with its institutional structure, the organization sustains its missionary, legal, pastoral and doctrinal aims. For example the movements of Catholic Action are born out of a missionary urgency arising from a contemporary challenge. They belong to the life of the church. The aim of missionary urgency remains, but the form produced by the challenge is provisional. It could be that to maintain it in the face of another challenge would prove disastrous. Lived out provisionally, i.e. constantly related to the challenge and the urgency, it proves its value for the church. The movements of Catholic Action have also gone on developing over against their own origin. For them to go on being faithful to forms defined in another situation would be absurd.

One could make identical comments about legal forms, pastoral organization and doctrinal decisions or expressions. In fact the aim of legality is to allow a non-violent co-existence between members of the same group or between heterogeneous groups. So legality is not an entity in itself but a function of the challenges made to co-existence. The prohibition against intercommunion between Christians of different confessions can have a beneficial significance in one situation, but there is no reason why the beneficial significance of the prohibition should be permanent; it is provisional. It may happen that it has pernicious effects when co-existence is sought within a confessional group and in relationship to other confessional groups. Pastoral strategies and organizations are not exempt from these mutations: they are even essential for a response to constantly changing challenges. Some will object in the case of doctrinal decisions or expressions. This case is more complicated, but it is quite similar. The forms expressed are not valid in themselves, but derive from relational systems and are therefore susceptible to variation in the coherence and relevance of these systems. Maintaining them in a fixed form serves to camouflage the questions which arise from new social relationships. The Roman document on the refusal to ordain women to the priesthood is a good example of this attachment to earlier forms and decisions. Passing judgment on the development of the idea of ministry which arose in the first centuries of the church is not of real interest. The debate is not about whether ancient options are well-founded, but about whether they are irrevocable. In fact to consider them irrevocable is to recognize that they are decisive for every other historical situation and therefore to accept that the particular context which led to such options has an exemplary and normative value. To justify the almost infinite weight of a particular decision the Catholic church appeals to the choices made by its founder, Jesus. In this particular case the authors of the document recognize that Jesus made absolutely no positive decisions on the matter. Jesus' exclusive choice of males is also made a matter of major importance, supporting a refusal to allow women a part in the priesthood and government of the church to come. It is said that the silence of Jesus is decisive, because elsewhere he shows himself to be sufficiently free towards the prevalent prejudices to have been able not to bow to the views of his contemporaries on the minor role of women. The ratification by subsequent tradition of this option of silence proves that it was taken as a positive and normative concern. The authors of the document do not think that the present legitimate movement for the liberation of women in society which lays claim to the same cultural, political and economic rights for them as for men can shake this interpretation: it does not question the matter of equal rights; it rejects it in the context of an unsurpassable difference which is confirmed by the fact that the Son became masculine and that those who must represent him within the communities cannot fail to take account of this historical fact. Hence the argument is based on a complex of historical facts which converge in one and the same rejection of a break in the tradition: the silence of Jesus, his maleness, the decision of the first Christians to exclude women from church government and priesthood. This complex takes on the status of a norm: certainly it is historical, but it determines in a definitive way the empirical structure of the church and confers on it a symbolism from which it cannot in any way depart. To the degree that social relationships change and women are integrated with the support of the law into positions where there is no distinction between the sexes, the Catholic community finds itself constrained to use doubtful anthropological reasons to justify its historical antipathy to giving women sacramental and hierarchical responsibility. Here the historical is opposed to the provisional to the degree that it has been elevated to being a normative order. The provisional keeps the historical historical even where it is not identical with it. What criterion of discernment makes it possible to make a distinction between the provisional, that is to say that which has a circumstantial significance and is mortal, and the historical, in which the significance becomes a structural norm? The Ultimate would not seem to me to provide this criterion for discernment: the symbolic is the mediator between the historically provisional and the structurally normative.

2. The symbolic order

The symbolic denotes a function and an objectivity. It denotes a function in that it is in the nature of human beings to live at a distance from 'things' or the 'real', since these are only the object of their desire within an exchange. The symbolic represents this function of integrating the massiveness of the 'real', designed as a vanishing point, into the social dialogue. It denotes an objectivity in that the production within the exchange takes many forms, but can always be grasped in a crystallized form. Thus language, rites, social structures and religious forms are products arising out of the symbolic exchange, constantly reinvented in this exchange, but objectified. Once it is withdrawn from this movement, the product which supports the exchange tends to fall back into the massiveness of the 'real'. It is at the heart of the dynamism of the exchange that its status is to be found. In this sense the symbolic is a process.

There seems to be no society which is not based on symbolic exchange. That makes them human. So the churches enter into this order. They do not escape the trend which appears once the movement of exchange dies down. The symbolic subsides into the massiveness of the 'real' and becomes an object for archaeology. It is also the provisional in the churches which protects the symbolic exchange and the symbolic exchange which supports the provisional. Without both these poles the churches are either stuck in immobility or are in turmoil and lack constancy. The immovable may claim to be the sign of the Absolute; it puts pressure on the inconstant by its rigidity. In fact the symbolic exchange within society does not call for immutable rites, hierarchies and doctrinal expressions, as if the stopping of social movement furthered a relationship with the divine. The symbolic exchange within the church postulates that forms, rites and social relationships are not fixed, so that the work of the Ultimate can be accomplished. So, far from absolutizing the concrete forms of ritual and church organization, the symbolic exchange claims that they are capable of transformation. That might seem paradoxical: the 'sacred' is thought to be immutable and to perpetuate the forms of its manifestation, so the rite would appear to be a stable datum. In the mobility of human actions, this stability ensures security.

In reality, formalizing the rite to the point of refusing to allow it to develop because that might make it betray what it signifies amounts in the long term to removing it from the symbolic order. The symbolic order requires that human exchanges should not be reduced to a utilitarian level. It is true that the commerce itself is never only mathematically rational. If the immutability of the rite makes it a safeguard against anxiety by virtue of barter with the sacred, it tends to be reduced to a utilitarian level because in the exchange between human beings it no longer reveals the Other who is involved and whom the utilitarian does not indicate. Moreover, if the rite is formal by virtue of its immobility, it robs the exchange of a temporal dimension, that tension towards a 'not yet' which marks all exchanges in the present as provisional.

This internal destruction of the symbolic order by formalism should not be an excuse for making the rite an expression which has to be reinvented on every occasion. The rite is only a rite if it exists before the occasion, controls it in some way, introduces those involved to another order than that of triviality and everyday utility. Attempts at destructuring the rite to give it life, like reducing the celebration of the last supper to a communal meal, have demonstrated the value of irony and the interrogative power of such a break with the rite. But these attempts only make sense, in other words involve the agents in a specific symbolic exchange, because this ironic presentation of the classical rite has come first and been contained in it. An ironic representation itself becomes a rite if it is repeated in a controlled form: in the case of the last supper it ceases to be a simple everyday fact. One can see how informal communities, tired of agitation, gradually ritualize their meetings, their organizations and their celebrations: if the exchange is not to descend to the triviality of everyday utility it reintegrates a ritual behaviour which marks out the distance between it and what is immediately perceptible. However, the irony was necessary to bring about an awareness of how the ritual repetition, closed as it is to the temporal dimension, and removed from the everyday world, would threaten the symbolic exchange. The irony reveals that the rite and its immutable formality is itself ironical since it brings to a miserable end the exchange that it should constantly reactivate. The prophetic criticism of sacrificial ritual in Israel has its roots in this perception of the ironical aspect of ineffectual repetition on exchanges between human beings. 'I want mercy and not sacrifice.' The irony lies in the fact that the rite takes the place of mercy, and therefore stands in the way of an evocation of infinite depths. The destructuring of rites in turbulent times is aimed at reintroducing a liveliness into human exchanges which they should have encouraged and which their formalism had hidden. But if the destructuring does not have a dialectical relationship with the rite, it has a tendency to rob the symbolic exchange of meaning in favour of an empty informality or a liturgy which is utilitarian and flat. The balance between formalism and utility is a difficult one to strike. The balance between the need for 'precession' and freedom of expression is hard to maintain: however, it is relevant to the truth of the symbolic exchange. A church cannot perpetuate irony or persist in formalism; in doing that it would lose its originality. In this sense the provisional preserves the rite from formalism, and the rite preserves the provisional from banality. This is the price to be paid if the symbolic exchange is not to fade away, and the churches are to be the places which indicate another dimension in exchanges between human beings, that to which scripture bears witness. The aim of their symbolic device is to further the social and communal practice of what is proclaimed, without reducing the content of the message.

The symbolic exchange brings out the excess that is concealed by the massiveness of the real and the positivity of the everyday. This excess can be seen and practised in three basic structures of the empirical churches: the sacrament, authority, and the Word. They demonstrate a dimension in everyday relations of which they are not the basis. The structures also determine the way in which symbolic exchange in the church is open to the kingdom.

The sacrament

The first structure which makes itself evident is the sacrament. It is a way into understanding the acknowledged link between the empirical churches and that to which they have a mission to bear witness, the kingdom.

The sacrament denotes the essential structure of the empirical church: it stamps on its everyday character, that is to say on its social relationships, a mark that originates in events which are an opening into the immanent process of history, and reveals the work of the Ultimate in the most immediate world. Human beings are doomed to die, but through being incorporated into the experience of Christ by the rite of water, the word and the gift of the Spirit are taken up in their pristine but precarious freshness by a people whose certainty about the future comes from Another: he has confronted death victoriously by not being afraid to risk his own fragile life to break the circle of that which works towards his practical domination in human relationships. So here human beings are symbolically incorporated into a vital and spiritual movement which encompasses them and goes beyond them, and by which their ethical, individual and social practice is inspired. Involved in a process the end of which they cannot control, since that end only comes to them through symbolic mime and the risk of decisions, the sacrament makes them witnesses of that for which they hope and of which they represent the partial fruits. Nor do they merely represent these first-fruits; they live them out in symbolic anticipation, since the meal in which they participate in memory of the martyrdom of Jesus and in the hope of his transforming coming brings together the people of brothers and sisters. Certainly they are aware of their failure to realize their hope of the reconciled city, but in fragile ways they bring about what they symbolize in the rite.

So the sacrament tips the everyday over into another sphere where the impossible claims to be possible. It is the excess which protests against the barriers imposed by flatness and immanence, which makes a rift in the greyness of everyday life and refuses the absolute of violence. A word risked on the basis of elements from the world and human communication bears witness to the work of the other communication, the covenant of which God has made his Christ the instrument and the witness by the specific gift of his Spirit. The flatness and the immanence open up: those who are sick and despairing hear in the rite which grasps them a word which offers them a future when the decrepitude of their strength apparently dooms them to the limits of mortality: men and women are not slaves of the desires within them which condemn them to be instruments of a biological process or prisoners of the moment; in Another they are the masters of their desire to be open to a communication to which the freedom of Christ summons them. The people is not an aggregate of groups and their struggles for survival and power, assuring them of places in the sun only by depriving others of theirs; it is built up on the sharing of bread, the multiplication of goods arising out of a refusal to establish one's own domination.

So the sacraments represent a symbolic device which takes hold of everyday life in its opaqueness with a view to making it express that of which it is the practical stake. The churches are networks of intercommunication concerned with something other than utility or survival. They recognize this something other in their origin to which the scripture bears witness, a focal point for their memory in their present that they try through the Spirit to snatch from its native entropy, and in the future that they live out under the sign of the promise. Without this symbolic structure which is made concrete in the social interplay defined by the rites, the churches would be an association for the improvement of individual and social life; they would not be that ambitious enterprise in which the craziest hopes, the cruellest insights, the most extravagant antipathies to the banality of evil and the excess of good are articulated: they would not denote the Spirit in the flesh but oppose it. The sacrament is this attempt to give practical expression in the fragility of the present moment of our relationships without devaluing what some cannot see, the over-abundant freedom of God in Christ. Without the sacrament the churches would only be the places for words or ethical associations. With it the beauty and serenity of another world are announced in the opaqueness and tragedy of time.

Is not this other world, announced in the symbolic network of the sacrament, denied by the all too human organization of the people? Does not the symbolic device lead to a justification of the hierarchical organization, i.e. to a denial of the brotherhood and sisterhood evoked by the term in historical anticipation? This brings us to the second aspect of the symbolic device in the churches: the form of authority.

Authority

The sacramental structure of the church involves everyday life in a symbolic network: it constrains it to provide an expression of what is at stake in it. But the sacramental structure, particularly in the Catholic church, determines the way in which it is organized: the sacrament of order provides the foundation for the form of authority, and it is as a function of this that the society of the church is structured. The episcopate is its axis: it defines in a downward direction priesthood of the second order and in an upward direction the collegiality and the presidency of the Bishop of Rome over it. The efforts of Vatican II to share the responsibilities of power (presbyteral councils and pastoral councils) do not diminish the hierarchical sacramental system. Pope and bishops have the last word when it comes to making decisions.

If we are to grasp the effect of this organization we must not forget its basis, the sacrament. The organization would in fact be capable of reform if it did not have a symbolic ambition. In that case reform would be simply a matter of analysing which system of government would be most suited for a particular new cultural and social situation. Without the symbolic dimension the organization of power is reduced to utility and efficiency. With the sacrament, this cannot happen. Providing as it does a basis for authority and legitimating the government, it signifies in the very structure of the church that authority is legitimated neither by the majority nor by consensus but by the one who symbolically institutes the sacrament, the Christ. The sacrament introduces an encounter in the society of the church between those who exercise their authority in place of Christ as a result of ordination and those who have not been given this representative function. Democracy works by another form of symbolism: the government of the people by the people presupposes that authority is delegated by the people and is therefore only legitimate to the degree that people give credit to it. The sacrament is the basis for an authority which derives its legitimation not from the people but from the one who makes it effective, the Christ. Thus the sacrament not only breaks everyday life apart in places where the Ultimate is at stake but represents within the social organization of the church a dimension which would seem to challenge the foundations of political legitimacy. Thus the easier it is to accept that the everyday expresses in the symbolic dimension more than it says of its own accord, the harder it would seem to admit that the difference between political society and the organization of the church could have a liberating power through its symbolism.

The sacrament which most opens up everyday life to the Ultimate is the eucharist. It takes up the communal and festive action of a meal and makes it the pledge and anticipation of universal sisterhood and brotherhood in a wealth of sharing. The churches are not mistaken about the importance of this symbolic act. Even those churches in which eucharistic celebrations have become rare for polemical reasons are restoring them to the centre of their liturgy. The problem is not caused by brotherly and sisterly sharing, which proclaims the kingdom, but by the presidency. The challenge to the Catholic idea of the eucharist is rooted in the appropriation of the presidency by priests and bishops who use this presidency to back up their social authority. Through the presidency, the eucharist moves from being a symbol of sisterhood and brotherhood to being a symbol of the hierarchy. The criticism of priesthood made by the Reformation has its roots in the reproduction of the liturgical form in society. Its universalization has seemed to favour the inauguration of a caste claiming uncontrolled power. At the Reformation we see a break in the symbolism: the Protestant churches maintain the symbolic expression of the everyday world while stressing the sisterly and brotherly aspects of eucharistic sharing; the Catholic church stresses the hierarchical symbolism which shifts the centre of gravity of the meal towards the sacrificial anamnesis. The present stress in the Catholic church on the brotherly and sisterly anticipation of the Ultimate through sharing relativizes the idea of sacrifice and puts in question the coherence between the hierarchical structure of the liturgy and the way in which it is represented in the church. The disputes which come about in the Catholic church partly arise from the symbolic contradiction between the sacrament which takes up everyday life and that which structures the organization of the church. Because of the exclusions for which it provides legitimation (the refusal to admit the laity to church government or to ordain women) the latter only entitles some members of the group to be able to lay claim to political responsibilities. The symbolism of the social structure of the Catholic church is selective, the symbol of the sacramentality which takes into itself the everyday world is non-exclusive. Paul's saying 'There is no longer Jew nor Greek... male nor female' applies to the latter. This slogan does not affect the social organization of the church: it is defined by relationships in the sphere of authority which no longer derive from the symbolism of sisters and brothers but from the conviction that human beings do not have control over their own salvation or liberation. Liberation by Another who does not enter into the framework of those who are to be saved proves so necessary that in symbolic form it takes precedence over that of brotherhood and sisterhood. The refusal to allow women to enter the priestly ministry originates in this symbolism, whatever may be the grounds from scripture or tradition used to legitimate it. Is it possible to go on governing the church according to two symbolic registers which seem to be contradictory? A great many believers think that the answer is no: they think that this schizophrenic symbolism was caused by social and cultural imperatives which no longer have any *raison d'être*. The liturgy, the place of the sacred, must no longer be the model for the organization of the church: the latter would benefit in every way from taking note of democratic developments in our Western society.

I have already touched on this question when discussing the institutional character of the church. Here it is accentuated by the social and cultural effects of a symbolism used within the church. In effect, to maintain the sacramental roots of the hierarchical structure of church society is either to separate it from other forms of social organization or to judge that these other forms are inferior.

To take the matter of separation first: the church should not be inspired by the development of social models: it offers a form for specific social relationships from which it would be as wrong to draw any political conclusions for the outside world as it would be to want to translate it into terms of secular requirements. We have two spheres which do not interpenetrate, since because of its sacramental and liturgical origin the model of the church cannot have any other point of application, and because they have only a rational origin the secular models cannot serve as a reference for symbolic ritualism. This is the perspective opened up by the document rejecting the admission of women to the priesthood: it fights for the social and political equality of men and women, but that applies only spiritually in the church; it has no legal and political truth because there is no symbolic support for it.

And then the matter of judgment: we know that the document to which I have alluded refrains from passing judgment on non-ecclesiastical democratic models. Where it does so, it encourages them, because since Pius XII the church has supported democracy as being the best form of government and social organization. In doing this it forgets too easily that the symbolism inferred by church organization has cultural effects: it is paradoxical to defend the equality of social and political rights of men and women in the secular world and to refuse them in the organization of the church

101

in the name of symbolism. The reasons put forward, whether they relate to tradition or to the supposed intentions of Jesus in this sphere, cannot get round the problem of the social effects of a society which claims to be a symbolic anticipation of the kingdom of God and which for this reason rejects all democratic forms of government. I find it difficult to see how what anticipates the kingdom in the symbolic structure of the church would not devalue the secular organization of society. Certainly it is argued that the aim of this hierarchical symbolism is to demonstrate that salvation comes from elsewhere, that it is not drawn from the grass roots. Not to express this origin would strike a blow at the origin of sisterhood and brotherhood symbolized by the sacrament of the eucharist. This sisterhood and brotherhood do not arise of their own accord but are the gift of the Spirit promised by Jesus. Not to incorporate this origin from elsewhere into the social structure would be to introduce a flaw or a break between the order of the sacrament and the order of the church: the hierarchy of authority is the consequence of the taking up of the everyday world into the sacrament. The everyday world can only produce what it may sketch out or desire. A transition through the liberating mediation of Another is necessary. The result is the hierarchical organization of the church. The church does not govern an economic and political sphere; it announces and anticipates that which surpasses all human power. So, far from striking a blow at the democratic organization of power, it denotes its lack of all power: it has no foundation in itself or in the people, since the law that it is charged to promulgate or apply does not derive its legitimacy simply from the majority or from consensus. Kant put this very well. So no authority could be sacred, but is under the judgment of Another, signified by the transcendence of the ethical law. Democracy is the best form of government by virtue of its specific acknowledgment of the relativity and secularity of its foundation. The hierarchical symbolism in the church brings out the equality of all human beings and therefore their lack of power over others in the paradox of a power which comes from elsewhere. The difference between the organization of secular society and that of the society of the church is represented in the contrast between their symbolism. Therefore, far from wanting to abolish it on the ground that the church must be relevant to the modern world, it is better to recognize this difference as basic. To equalize these two societies on the basis of a single model would not bring out what is latent in the secular and would trivialize what is specific in the church. Thus, the argument goes, the rooting of the hierarchical symbolism of the church in the sacrament does not devalue social democratic organization but reveals its foundations: brotherly and sisterly co-existence worthy of the name only exists by reason of the Word of Another who transcends the relationship.

However, this argument must not too easily sweep aside the possible social effects of this symbolism. The transposition of the symbolic ordering of the liturgy to the social organization of the church exercises pressure to fix provisional data in sacrality: so it does not encourage attention to the real situation and the perception of those who may possibly hear the gospel; it leads to a conception of evangelization along the lines of the liturgical model. In short, the domination of the liturgical model eliminates the heuristic character of all pastoral work and all ethics. The liturgical model ritualizes decisions of a moral and political kind.

The churches of the Reformation saw the dangers in the social organization of the community: authority based on the sacrament favours an indisputable hierarchy and this then appropriates to itself the Word of God of which it should be the servant. Would the subordination of word to sacrament, the introduction of a critical authority into the symbolic order, exorcise the potentially perverse character of the difference between church society and secular society? It is this last point that we have still to elucidate: the status of the Word in the symbolic order buttressing the provisional nature of the churches.

The Word

The symbolic order as we have seen it in the Catholic church binds three elements into a synthesis: the sacrament, governmental authority and the Word. I have suggested that experience leads us to put a necessary distance between the sacrament and government. The foundation of the one on the other leads to a structuring of the social organization of the church on the basis of the liturgical order and thus to a sacralization of the authority of the priestly caste. There is a risk of even greater excess if statements of doctrine are grounded in the sacrament; in short, if the symbolic order of church communication, of which the word is an essential element, is rooted in and justified by the social gap which the sacrament of order sets up. So is it not necessary to reverse the movement and recognize in a Word over which no caste has control the declaration signifying the provisional, circumstantial and partial nature of the sacrament?

We know the choice made by the churches which emerged from the Reformation when they were confronted with the grave consequences of inflation of the sacrament: the church ceases to be a people bringing into the everyday world the unheard-of dimension of the kingdom and becomes a hierarchical society in which the caste sacralized by the sacrament holds absolute power of interpretation and orientation, mobilizing the memory of the group against the freedom which the gospel gives to all. The dilution of the bond between the sacrament, church government and the Word opens up a sphere for general responsibility. This sphere is guaranteed by the Word itself since the Word is not the present fruit of enlightenment or the effect of the ideology of a pressure group but the actuality of scripture confirmed by the gift of the Spirit. Hence what in the Catholic church led to a break with secular society by reason of its hierarchical structure no longer has any effect here. There is no specific structure of the church based on the sacrament, but a particular demand for behaviour which the sacrament makes specific and which the Word introduces. The Word does not create a caste or specialists in its interpretation and its social effects: it calls on all believers to bring out in the opaqueness of the everyday world the dimension of brotherhood and sisterhood and the Ultimate dimension of the kingdom: the freedom of the divine gift. The churches of the Reformation do not abolish the symbolic order for the benefit of ethical platitudes; they displace it because they reverse the relationship in the synthesis and thus ground the creative work of the community in the world on the Word actualized in scripture by the Spirit.

Despite regrettable historical trends, the Catholic church has not thought it necessary to adopt the Reformed option; it has maintained the link between the three elements in the symbolic order – the sacrament, authority and the Word – giving the first the role of providing a structural foundation for the functioning of the two others. Hence for the Catholic church, the sacrament separates it as church, that is to say that it differentiates it from all other civil or secular societies; it draws the attention of these societies to the otherness needed for maintaining their incompleteness, for guaranteeing their vitality. The authority for government instituted within it by the sacrament bears witness to the lack inherent in all authority since it is not based on itself, on the people or on the majority. It thus indicates the limitation of all power in the empirical. Finally the third element, the Word, bears witness to the same lack of human discourse since it does not derive its ultimate truth from itself but from a spokesman for whom there can be no substitute. Hence the sacrament which inaugurates the church, legitimates its authority and opens up the way to discourse with the Other guarantees in social structures that the society of the church society will not collapse in an imitation of secular society. The apparent rigidity of the Catholic structure gives it prophetic force.

The Catholic choice is one of synthesis. The symbolic order into which it is integrated comes from Another and this derivation is expressed in the relational structure of the three elements mentioned above. The Reformed concern to involve the Word throughout on the grounds that this will provide a guarantee against the drift towards hierarchy and its interests runs the risk of destroying the symbolic order for the benefit of an ethical voluntarism, even if this ethic is one of free gift. The trivialization of celebration, the reduction of the language of intercommunication to the one Word bears witness to the dangers produced by the disintegration of the symbolic order of the church. But can this Catholic option be a balanced one without the question raised by the other option which constantly bears witness to the way in which it may be drifting?

To fill out my comments I have taken as an example doctrinal authority in Catholicism. This authority does not exist independently of the sacramental institution by which a Christian enters the college of bishops. But the sacramental institution is a possible and not a sufficient condition: the bond of communion of which the eucharist is certainly the symbol is indispensable. Doctrinal authority is secondary to this bond. Thus the ministry of unity which was accorded to the Bishop of Rome towards the local churches has priority over that of orthodoxy. That is why the Bishop of Rome must preside over communion between the churches, and ensure that this is not an empty proclamation but a specific reality, that it has a role in this exchange of a charisma which prevents it from leading to error in the confession of Christ. Hence it must be recognized that the symbolic element of the Word as an indication that witness is not possessive in its place is equally secondary in relation to the bond of communion: it can be heard to be true within the circle of this bond, and it has authority in work towards this bond. It is the definitive form of the quest or the pursuit of the institution of this bond of communion which verifies the aim of the sacrament, the authenticity of the Word and the legitimacy of the authority. Neither the sacrament nor the Word are enough to legitimate the authority if the practice does not aim at what the sacrament and the Word point to symbolically: the manifestation in the everyday world of the movement of communion sparked off by the action of Christ and the gift of the Spirit.

It will be seen that this interpretation of the symbolic order recognizes ecumenical work as the scarlet thread which keeps together the three elements that differentiate the empirical churches from secular organizations.

In fact ecumenism begins from the observation that the multiplicity of churches shows that communion can only be potential: it is not given, but a task to pursue. The multiplicity of churches is not so much a negative sign as the specific indication of the multiplicity of the ways to unity in time. This multiplicity of the churches is thought to be negative by a church which aims at reducing the others to itself. Ecumenism as a task and an opening up of thought begins where this multiplicity is welcomed in a positive way, not as a reduction but as authentic and not just legal communion. Obsession with the sacrament or its exclusiveness, like domination by the Word or the accentuation of legal authority, leads to mutual dismemberment in the name of the ideal of brotherhood. The symbolic order that sacrament, Word and authority aim to sustain is broken for the benefit of a legal concern for unity, in other words a feigned communion. It is pursued elsewhere by successive exclusions: the brotherhood aimed at appears only after violence.

The ministry of unity works at the heart of this multiplicity so that the Word of peace proclaimed by Jesus does not destroy its potentiality for the benefit of one church which then becomes imperialistic. So it seems to me inconceivable that communion could be a legal outcome tied to a privilege outside intercommunion between the churches. The present multiplicity prevents the symbolic order from transforming itself into legal imperialism, a violent form of the truth putting itself into practice.

The Catholic church, accustomed by its history to accuse all who disagree with it of breaking communion, and impelled to practise the truth in the form of legal unity, feels a malaise over the questioning from the ecumenical world. On the one hand it does not want to reject this questioning and even wants to take it seriously, but, certain of its structural harmony with the proclamation of the truth, it thinks that the way of unity is a way of reintegration. On the other hand it hesitates before becoming involved in the destabilization which ecumenical practice produces with respect to its image of unity and its symbolism.

It is true that the multiplicity of churches, by not determining the form of unity, and therefore leaving a great many possibilities open, develops to the full the symbolism of communion based on the unity of sacrament, authority and Word. That can be seen in specific rites, decisions and expressions. The multiplicity of churches, by introducing a multiplicity of interpretations, paralyses this movement towards making unity specific and blurs it. Definitions, in other words exclusions, are necessary for unity to become tangible. How can the Catholic church accept a symbolic order which does not postulate the exclusion of multiplicity but impels it to continue as a condition of the possibility of communion? Perhaps it might be enough not to judge that the other church is a negation of one's own, but the limit which indicates that it is not the kingdom or the Ultimate. The multiplicity of churches would then be the historical form of the work of the Ultimate.

3. The work of the Ultimate

The churches are worthy of this name only if they are not associations for seeing to spiritual needs but witnesses to the Unexpected. By Unexpected I mean the Ultimate: its model is the Easter event. The one whom all thought dead affirmed that he was alive. The churches are witnesses to this living one. Not like an anecdote relating a strange and miraculous fact of the past but by proclaiming that the everyday is about this life which destroys death.

The objection to this hope is serious: our history unfolds in the grip of violence and death proves victorious. The churches represent small groups, which contradict one another and are sometimes even contradictory in themselves. They are aware of being provisional in their forms, imperfect or open to criticism in their conduct, hesitant in their options. Their members cannot lay claim to a better life than that of outsiders. Nor is their visible character the anticipation of the kingdom, in the form in which it is celebrated, in its social life or in its spiritual value. The churches are not icons of the kingdom. However, since their social structures call for a change of conduct, the churches are not dumb: they support a symbolic order which opens up the everyday world to a dimension of freedom and communion which is like the trace of God in Christ.

The work of the Ultimate denotes a limit and a hope.

It denotes a limit: since the symbolic order of the church opens up the everyday world to the Ultimate it forces the church to accept its provisional character. This constraint is specific: it is evident from the multiplicity of churches. None is immersed in the secular to the point of no longer being capable of standing out from it; none has taken on the secular to the point of transsubstantiating it. But by their activities all tend to seek to abolish separation in order to hasten the hour of the kingdom: their mediation and their multiplicity keep them from succumbing to this temptation. For when they do succumb to it they use violence, and their actions, too conformed to the violence of history, make it evident that they are not identical with the kingdom. When they enter into ecumenical negotiation, their renunciation of violence ensures that they personally are identified with the kingdom. To create a bond without exclusion suggests as a starting point a truth experienced as a limit but given as a hope.

The work of the Ultimate also denotes a hope: the work of hope is not to crystallize the action of the kingdom in an empirical model, but by the gift of the Spirit to persuade a church not to follow the trend towards exclusion which is as it were the natural law of the group. That is why the slow reversal, which is taking place in the history of churches and beyond them in the history of religions, of an ideology of conquest by combat, as if God were a war lord, and its replacement by a practice of negotiation moving towards possible communion, is transforming the situation and the politics of the churches. But what the Spirit is inspiring is in a way a movement against nature.

It seems that the natural movement of societies is to form satellites round a centre. Equilibrium is practised and thought of in terms of the centre: it represents the unifying factor. If the centre loses its power to unify, the system breaks up or disappears. The history of the church illustrates this movement. Out of a number of centres one gradually comes to predominate, to the degree that rivalries over hegemony break up the system. The Catholic church thought that it had to increase pressure from the centre to maintain empirical unity. But this constant pressure has gone beyond tolerable limits: the divisions at the Reformation are the result of this concern for hegemony. The attempt made to recreate the system by force (as in the Wars of Religion) simply produced greater dissensions. Ecumenism represents this original development of no longer treating relations from a real or imaginary centre but as a plurality. Can this originality be maintained? Will not the ideology of unity prove too powerful? Will it allow discussion to the point of negotiation towards communion without imposing the claims of a centre?

The work of the Ultimate is spontaneously confused with the imperialism of the centre or with the rediscovery of a centre. It is imagined almost naturally that the kingdom comes through the empirical manifestation of a centre which draws all to it. Now a parable, a reply made by Jesus and the image of the activity of the Spirit should warn us against this tendency.

The parable is that of the wheat and the tares. The apostles were in a hurry to introduce eschatological clarity. They wanted unification at any price. Jesus warned them that they would destroy the wheat. The transparency of acting from a common centre of interest would imperil the aims of the kingdom.

Jesus gave his reply while the disciples were going through a Samaritan village and were badly received. They wanted to exterminate it with fire from heaven. Jesus warned them against this zeal. They were to let the Samaritans go their own way. They were not to impose their views on them and above all they were not to punish them for their disagreements.

The image of the Spirit appears in Jesus' remarks to Nicodemus that no one knows where the Spirit comes from or where it goes, and to the Samaritan woman that there was no longer any central place for worshipping God.

Jesus rejects the idea of the dominant centre. And I see in the new ecumenism one of the forms of the work of the Ultimate in the churches.

I have said 'one of the forms', because I do not forget that the prophetic presence in the world, welcome for the outcast or support for the poor, are indications of this work. But this work would be useless for the churches if it were done in a competitive or violent attitude. As long as the plurality of the churches is thought of as a sinful situation and not as a structural basis for their relationship with the kingdom there is a risk that the demon of unitary and imperialist compulsion will be reborn. Moreover, paradoxically it is in the positive acceptance of plurality that the churches, by their capacity for communion, bear witness to the Ultimate. Their provisional situation is the criterion for their authenticity. The symbolic order finds its truth in the practice of communion between the churches.[1]

Postscript

'Economy and theology are equivalent explanations of history. Or rather I should say that they are omnivalent. The omnivalence is secured by violence. Theology, violence and economy run on the same lines, or rather they occupy the same space, by which I mean all space.'[1]

These comments by M.Serres are at first sight surprising. However, they describe the demon of theology: to consider everything from a point judged to be central and unifying because it is God. This procedure leads to violence, since everything has willy-nilly to be forced into a perspective which rejects the other perspectives as illegitimate. God is the name substituted for the central point. In ecclesiology that is the ideal church. For the theologian, ideal church denotes normative church: so it defines the legitimate structure and activity of the empirical churches. The true church is that which is least removed from the ideal definition. Theoretically and empirically it then becomes the model to which the other churches must conform. Violence is on the doorstep: the ideal brings it into being and legitimates it. M.Serres is right: omnivalence engenders violence. The wars between the Christian churches were not only matters of impulse; they were rationally justified if only one church is legitimate, i.e. has a right to exist. The right may be enjoyed only by the church which is least removed from the ideal in its structure and activity. On the basis of their confession, theologians show that this is the case with their church. They open hostilities by the very dynamic of their thought.

I have tried to banish this type of thought by giving multiplicity its due and by rejecting any form of ideal church as an imperative model, seen in the Catholic form as a symbolic and dynamic order of community. The historicity and provisional character of the churches, including the Catholic church, ensure that the theoretical concern is not a noble illusion. However, I cannot disguise the fact that the ecumenical aim in theology clashes with well-established traditions and convictions, honoured with the label of 'sacred'. Still, I think that taking into account an ecclesiology with a multiple system will help to cure the temptation to violence inherent in the idea of unitary structure and centralizing practice. This is not a coincidence if the papal function is the cross of ecumenism. Thought and practice in a multiple system call for radical conversion and not destruction of its practice and theorizing.

I do not despair of the possibility that contributions to another idea of the church will allow the abandonment of a process of centralization and make it possible to renounce an imperialistic idea of unity in favour of a ministry of unity associated with the *de facto* multiplicity of the churches.

Notes

I The Churches and History

1. Cf. Y.M.J.Congar, *Lay People in the Church*, Geoffrey Chapman 1969.

2. The note by the French Cardinals and Archbishops dated March 1946, *DC* 1946, col.743. It is worth studying the development and the significance of the term 'mandate' in Congar, op.cit., 333ff. Fr Congar, who ends with the post-war discussions, does not perhaps stress sufficiently the ecclesiological ambiguity of the official origin of Catholic Action.

3. Text in Abbott, *The Documents of Vatican II*, 14–96; Austin Flannery, *Vatican Council II. The Conciliar and Post-Conciliar Documents*, Costello Publishing Corporation and Fowler Wright Books 1981, 350-423.

4. H.Legrand, 'L'avenir des ministères, bilan, défis, tâches', in *Le Supplement*, February 1978, 21ff.; 'Les ministères dans l'Eglise locale', in *Initiation à la pratique de la théologie* III, *Dogmatique 2*, Editions du Cerf, Paris 1983, 181-274; E.Schillebeeckx, *The Church with a Human Face*, SCM Press and Crossroad Publishing Company, New York 1985.

5. H.Küng, *The Church*, Search Press 1969.

6. The term entropy denotes a mathematical function expressing the principle of the degradation of energy.

7. Y. Congar, 'The Church, one, holy, catholic, apostolic', in *Mysterium Salutis* ('Dogmatics of Salvation History', IV, 15). I am afraid that the account in J.Hoffmann, 'L'Eglise et son origine', in *Initiation à la pratique de la théologie* III, *Dogmatique 2*, Editions du Cerf 1984, 53-131, has not been subjected to a similar criticism.

8. M.-J.Bérère, R.Dufour, D.Singles, *Et si on ordonnait des femmes?*, Paris 1982. This aspect is brought out particularly clearly in this book.

9. It must be noted that the Reformation is rooted in the Pauline proclamation of Christian freedom. The Reformation churches do not always draw the specific consequences of this.

10. The Pelagian controversy was over the problem of the free gift of salvation, and took place at the beginning of the fifth century. Pelagius taught that human beings could achieve salvation simply by their ethical

merits, and therefore by their own efforts. Augustine recalled, sometimes bluntly, the initiative of God and the free gift of his salvation.

11. Instruction of the Congregation for the Doctrine of Faith, *DC* LXXVII, no.1717, 7 December 1980, 1107-13.

12. P.Gibert, *La Bible. A la naissance de l'histoire*, Paris 1979, 339-436.

13. In particular I am thinking of the episode of Ananias and Sapphira (Acts 5.1-11). The text emphasizes the sin of these two Christians and omits to see in their death the effect of the ideal of perfection on a historical community.

14. Eusebius' *The History of the Church* is available in English translation in an edition published by Penguin Books, 1965.

15. Speech made in the basilica of Tyre, op.cit., 383-401.

16. One could put suggest that the disappearance of millenarianism in the fourth century coincided with the conversion of the empire: the time had then come.

17. Augustine's *City of God* is good evidence of these contradictions. It was written in the fifth century.

18. Pastoral constitution *Gaudium et Spes*, Abbott,199–308; Flannery, 903-1001.

19. J.-B.Metz, *La Foi dans l'histoire et dans la société. Essai de théologie fondamentale pratique*, Paris 1979, 176-92, 230-56.

II The Churches and the Institution

1. Among the large number of works on this question I should mention E.Poulat, *Une Église ébranlée, changement, conflit, continuité de Pie XII à Jean-Paul II*, Paris 1980; – *Massa e Meriba. Itinerari di fede nella Storia delle communità di base*, Turin 1980; *Una chiesa senza preti*, Varese 1981; P.Warnier, *Nouveaux témoins de l'Église, les communautés de base*, Paris 1981.

2. I note that the article 'Institutions' in the *Thesaurus* of the *Encyclopaedia Universalis*, which appeared in 1968 (vol.19, col.950) is very anti-institutional. The aim of institutions it gives as subjection. The study of institutions comes within an analysis of power. Thus the problem raised by institutions is expressed as: 'How can human beings be domesticated?' For this to happen, every institution produces a canonical statement which rejects as deviants all those who do not make an act of allegiance towards it.

3. In *L'Église après Vatican II, Dynamisme et prospective, Actes du colloque international de Bologne, 1980*, ed. Giuseppe Alberigo, Paris 1981, 149-85.

4. Abbott, 152; Flannery, 14.

5. *De Controversis* II, Liber 3, *De Ecclesia militante*, ch.2, *Definitio Ecclesiae*, Naples 1857, 75.

6. Abbott, 14–96; Flannery, 350-426.

7. Constitution *Lumen Gentium*, §10, 11, 12, Abbott, 26–30; Flannery 360-4.

114

8. Ibid., § 10, Abbott, 27; Flannery 360-1.

9. Ibid., §9, Abbott, 24–6; Flannery 359-60.

10. Ibid.

11. Ibid., §15-16, Abbott, 33–5; Flannery 366-8.

12. This reform foreseen since the end of Vatican II has yet to reach its end.

13. The experience of synods is perhaps too recent to provide an answer to these questions, but it shows that the bishoprics have little autonomy over against the central power and that their representation of the Christian people is ambiguous.

14. B.Franck, *Vers un nouveau droit canonique*, Paris 1983. The author worked on the definitive schema, but not on the text that was promulgated.

15. Cf. section 1 of this chapter.

16. *Receptio* is understood to mean the active welcome or the rejection by Christian people of the decisions of the authorities.

17. It was over the mass celebrated by John-Paul II on 4 March 1983 at Managua and his homily (*DIAL* 848, 14 April, 1983 and the review *Jésus*, 37, June 1983).

18. *Lumen Gentium* §25, Abbott, 47–50; Flannery 379-81.

19. Romans 13.1.

20. *Inter Insigniores*, on the admission of women to the priesthood, *DC* 59, 1977, 158-64, and *Sacerdotalis Coelibatus* of Paul VI, *AAS* 59, 1967, 91-104.

21. The arguments of those opposed to *Inter Insigniores* are not always clear on this point, cf. L. and A.Swidler (ed.), *Women Priests. A Catholic Commentary on the Vatican Declaration*, Paulist Press, New York 1977.

22. The document promulgated by the French bishops meeting at Lourdes in 1973, *Tous responsables*, Paris 1973.

23. To the episode at Managua recalled in n.17 must be added the tense dialogue with Sister Theresa Kane in the USA in October 1979 (*DC* LXXVI, no.1173, 4 November 1979, 840).

24. It is worth reading on this question G.Thils, *La primauté pontificale. La doctrine de Vatican I. Les voies d'une revision*, Gembloux 1972; *L'infaillibilité pontificale. Source, conditions, limites*, Gembloux 1979; H.Küng, *Infallible?*, Fount Books 1974; Y. Congar, 'Infaillibilité et indefectibilité', *RSPT* 54, 1970, 601-18; J.-M.-R. Tillard, *L'évêque de Rome*, Paris 1982.

25. Küng, op.cit., and Tillard, op.cit., have notably stressed this point.

26. L.M. Chauvet, *Du symbolique au symbole*, Paris 1979; R.Didier, *Les sacrements de la foi, la Pâque dans ses signes*, Paris 1975.

III   The Church, a Mystical Reality

1. The word *eschaton* denotes the ultimate reality.

2. In *Encyclopedia Universalis* 16, 557, Paris 1968. I am indebted to this article for the description given here.

3. There is an interesting note on millenarianism by G.Bardy in his edition of St Augustine's *City of God*, Paris 1960, 768-71.

4. A convenient translation of *The City of God* is published by Penguin Books, 1972.

IV   *The Provisional, the Symbolic and the Kingdom*

1. Compare with what is said here J.Hamer, 'Dix thèses sur l'Église comme communion', *Nova et Vetera* LIX, 3, July-September 1984, 16.

Postscript

1. Michel Serres, *Rome. Les fondations*, Paris 1984, 42.

DATE DUE

DEC 2 1 1999			

HIGHSMITH   #LO-45220